SWEET DREAMS:

Fourteen Ways to Sleep at Will

GEORGE BEMIS BELTING, J.D.
and ELIZABETH KUHL BELTING

DRAKE PUBLISHERS INC.

NEW YORK · LONDON

Published in 1977 by
Drake Publishers, Inc.
801 Second Avenue
New York, N.Y. 10017

Library of Congress Cataloging in Publication Data

Belting, George.
        Sweet dreams.

        1. Insomnia. I. Belting, Elizabeth, joint author.
II. Title.
RC548.B44   616.8' 49   77-6185
 ISBN 0-8473-1609-2

Printed in the United States of America

CONTENTS

Introduction / 5

Chapter

I	Facts about Sleep / 7	
II	Get the Jungle Out of Your System / 17	
III	Sleeping Pills Do Make You Different / 25	
IV	Gateways to Approach Sleep Technique / 33	
V	Concentrative Self-Suggestion for Sleep / 42	
VI	The Kelly Method / 48	
VII	The Jacobson Methods / 56	
VIII	Dr. Fink's Method / 65	
IX	Meditation into Sleep / 70	
X	The Roon Technique for Sleep / 77	
XI	Self-Hypnotism into Sleep / 81	
XII	Biofeedback for Sleep / 90	
XIII	The Wallace Method / 94	
XIV	Electrosleep Treatment / 103	
XV	Zen Meditation for Sleep / 105	
XVI	Dr. Pai's System for Sleep / 110	
XVII	The Steincrohn Technique / 113	
XVIII	Yoga Methods / 116	
XIX	Body Charting for Sleep / 120	
XX	Sleep Equipment / 123	
XXI	Author's Comments / 125	

Introduction

You can sleep at will.

In different ways, different authorities and experts on sleep have found methods to solve the problems of sleeplessness which come from stresses and psychosomatic ills. The methods that have been evolved provide untroubled sleep, relaxation and build up your confidence in mastering control of your body and mind. These solutions provide a guide for the range of sleep troubles.

The various methods developed by these world authorities are described for you so that you can use and adopt them. They tell you how to handle occasional sleeplessness and what to do for chronic pre-sleep, mid-sleep or post-sleep insomnia. You can make the choice of method, combine methods to suit your needs, or try alternative techniques until you are satisfied. All remedies do not work for all people. You pick the strategy that works for you.

In our stress filled modern society, not one person has been able to avoid an occasional distressing period of tension, anxiety and the resulting insomnia. This book offers scientifically tried and tested techniques to combat your problem.

Simple, basic instructions will enable you to learn and practice the plainly described techniques. Your benefits should start immediately. The results will bring not only satisfying normal sleep to your nights, but renewed energy and effectiveness to your days.

Chapter I

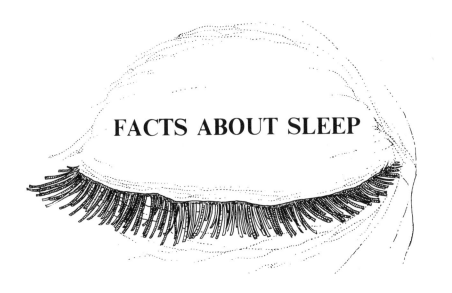

FACTS ABOUT SLEEP

Sleep is a problem

According to a nationwide survey, fifty-two percent of Americans report that they suffer from loss of sleep. Not only are such persons disgusted at not getting to sleep, but their nights are followed by various disabilities of performance and enthusiasm. These disabilities affect their success with their family, their fellow workers, their employment, their attractiveness, their health and their length of life. Studies and tests leave no doubt that loss of sleep does cause inefficiency, both mentally and physically. It also causes physical errors and mistakes of judgment. Total deprivation of sleep causes death. You can live much longer without food than you can without sleep. Efforts to find the rumored person who does not sleep have always failed.

The master controller of sleep

Deep in the center of the bottom of the brain is a small area called the hypothalamus. From direct experimentation on animals, plus the discoveries resulting from injuries or disease in the human brain, knowledge has developed which shows that the hypothalamus and a chain of adjacent related areas of the brain exercise direct control over your sleep. These same areas, which were developed very early in the evolutionary process, also give the directions that control temperature, perspiration, metabolism, pulse, depth of breathing, glandular secretions and other basic activities over which you ordinarily have little or no conscious control. These same areas exercise much of the control over hunger, cycle of moods and sexual manifestations.

It is the hypothalamus that gives the orders to sleep. For instance, sometimes your hypothalamus gives the direction for a nap during the day: at your desk, watching TV or while driving your automobile. Accidentally, you have set up the conditions in the brain for going to sleep. You may resist the sleep, in which case, you may get repeated tiny sleeps called micro-sleep. These may happen to you with your eyes wide open and without your knowledge. You may give in to the signal to sleep, doze or even lie down for a nap. These daytime sleep signals are normal and more frequent after the loss of sleep.

Narcolepsy

The signals from the brain to go to sleep are due to chemistry in the sleep area. They can be amazingly sudden. When these signals to go to sleep during the daytime are regular and expectable, they are called narcolepsy. They appear to be misplaced bits of sleep, lasting from seconds up to minutes. They have been sometimes mistakenly identified with catalepsy, but are totally different. In narcolepsy, the person has almost a total muscular relaxation. He may retain some consciousness of what is going on, but he cannot move a muscle. There is a tendency for narcolepsy to occur in persons who are chronically drowsy. Employers sometimes charge such a person with sleeping on the job.

The onset of the misplaced sleep appears with some regularity, tending to increase in occurrence as the years go on. Unfortunately, it seems to occur during increased excitement such as laughter, anger, while driving a car or making love. The condition is still not well understood. Treatment is to prescribe stimulants to stay awake. At present there is no known cure.

Spying on the brain

A great breakthrough in discovering the nature of sleep occurred in April, 1952, when a Chicago graduate student, studying under Dr. Nathaniel Kleitman, was taking electroencephalograms of sleeping subjects to measure electrical impulses produced in the brains of the subjects.

An electroencephalogram is made by a pen on a slowly moving roll of paper. The pens are activated by enormously amplified electric charges received from electric contacts attached to spots on the body and head. Thousands of persons have spent the night in sleep laboratories in the United States attached to the electrodes of encephalograph machines. In the course of one night, over a quarter of a mile of paper will show the record of changes in the electric charges received from the electrodes on the body. The electrodes are taped behind the ears, on the chin, on the forehead, on the nostril and on the top of the head. They measure the total sum of the thousands of electrical bursts per second coming from the brain. They also measure breathing, pulse, temperature and eye movement.

Eugene Aserinsky noticed that when the electric charges moved the pen up and down on the paper in a certain way, there always appeared to be darting eye movements. The movement of the pen up and down on the paper made lines that resemble waves. The experimenters came to refer to them as brain waves.

These electroencephalogram experiments have enabled scientists to reveal the secrets of sleep. The classification of brain waves not only tell the type of sleep you are in from minute to minute, but they also can tell whether you had an alcoholic drink or sleeping pills in the period before sleep. The encephalogram is useful in diagnosing mental disorders.

The stages of sleep

Researchers of sleep discuss six stages, the threshold; followed in order by stage one; deeper and deeper stages called stage two, stage three and stage four. The final classification is called REM for Rapid Eye Movement. REM is the most interesting of all the stages. The REM stage is part of the second and successive stage one periods. A complete cycle of all the stages lasts around ninety minutes on the average. The cycles follow each other for a total of four or more cycles each night. All of the stages are required for healthful sleep.

During the threshold stage your are in a period of comfortable relaxation. You may have the sensation of floating into and out of light sleep one or more times. You are without concentrated thought. Your senses are dulled; your residual muscular tension is decreasing. The electrically measured brain waves number about twelve per second, measured in millionths of a volt. It is during this period that you may experience the muscular jerk as the relaxation progresses, causing you to be aroused for a moment. It occurs at the onset of sleep. Although it is a signal that sleep has begun, everyone denies that he has been asleep.

In stage one the electrical rhythm of pulse in the brain is a little slower than during the threshold. You can still be awakened very easily by touch, sound or light. If you are awakened, you will not remember that you were asleep. Changes are taking place throughout your body with decreasing pulse, blood pressure, breathing, muscle tension, secretions, temperature and metabolism. If you wake later in stage one you will not remember having been in a dream. The period of time spent in stage one getting deeper into sleep will last around twenty minutes.

Stage two is the continuation of the slowly decreasing level of bodily functions started in the threshold. The brain wave pulses are slower, the eyes cannot see if they are opened and much louder sound would be required to awaken you. The nose becomes drier and the reflexes for coughing and sneezing are quieted. The bladder and intestines are relaxed, although kidney function and digestion continue. The eyes are relaxed enough to begin to roll. Nevertheless part of the brain is awake at all times. That part of the brain is never completely asleep as it stands watch against danger. The brain is aware enough to keep you from falling out of bed, as well as to direct the muscles to pull up the covers or turn off the alarm clock.

Stage three continues the declining brain and body activity to a lower level as you descend deeper into sleep. At this point the brain waves have a big wide shape, showing electric pulses occurring about one per second. Waking from this stage rarely results in awareness of any kind of dream vision at all. Although the pulses of electricity are less frequent in their rhythm, they are bigger when they do come.

The amount of time spent in each cycle of stages remains at close to ninety minutes each, but the level of body activity continues to decline slightly, around four hours from the onset of sleep, reaching its lowest level sometime between three and five o'clock in the morning. Blood pressure is down ten to thirty points, pulse down ten to thirty beats and metabolism down fifteen percent.

In stage four the body functions decline about as far as they will go. You are as close to total oblivion as you will get. The brain waves are long, slow, wandering and irregular. The stage lasts around forty minutes in the first cycle of the night and decreases about ten minutes with each cycle of ninety minutes. In the final cycle of the night, it may be skipped entirely. The total amount of stage four sleep you need each night remains quite stable at between twenty and twenty—five percent of the night's sleep.

Although stage four is the period of deepest sleep, it is also the time when sleepwalking occurs in the one percent of the population. It is the period in which sleep talking, sleep screaming or nightmares occur. Because of the almost total relaxation present in stage four, it is also the period when bed-wetting occurs. During the nightmare the body experiences real panic, with a heart beat as high as 170 having been recorded.

Stage four is associated with repair and rebuilding of the body. The need for stage four sleep increases a little following a day of exercise or heavier than usual labor. It increases after illness comes or when feeling physically tired. It lasts longer in manual laborers. Its length decreases when a manual laborer moves from heavy labor to sedentary work. Cell replacement in the body which occurs in stage four, is faster during sleep. The mending of broken bones is related to the amount of stage four sleep.

Although amazing new knowledge has developed about all stages of sleep, it is the REM stage that attracts the most attention. The numerous projects of research into the REM stage proves that almost one hundred percent of those who are awakened during this stage can remember a dream vividly. Some dreams last for many minutes, and occur at nearly the same rate of progress that the events would occur in real life.

It is evident from electric burst firing up from the brain that feverish mental activity is going on. These bursts of electrical activity in the brain can usually be related to events the subject can remember when he is suddenly awakened from his dream. The areas of the brain brought into play are not only the sleep center areas but most areas of the brain.

In the intensity of the dreaming activity, not only do the eyes dart about under the closed eyelids, but the vocal cord muscles show tiny movements as if speaking. In deaf-mutes the REM stage produces tiny twitches of the fingers.

Loss of REM sleep, whether in humans or mammals, results in two things. The brain is very sensitive to the loss of REM sleep and seeks to replace the loss at the earliest possible occasion by having the REM stage come sooner, more often or last longer. Because sleeping pills partly or totally may deprive a person of the occurrence of the REM stage of sleep, those withdrawing from sleeping pills can have the experience of almost continuous REM sleep.

Second, the loss of REM sleep develops irritability, confusion, lack of energy, decreased learning ability and lower IQ. The testing of animals, as well as the observation on humans after several days of deprivation of the REM stage, shows that hallucinations, inability to speak coherently and lack of concentration will occur.

The first REM period of the night is about ten minutes long, but in each succeeding sleep cycle, there is an additional ten minutes of REM. During the later cycles of the night, there is much more of the dream stage of sleep. This increase in REM roughly corresponds to the decrease in stage four sleep in each successive cycle of the night. The total amount of time spent in REM sleep is increased even more as a result of extraordinary mental activity or emotional stress that occurs during the previous day.

Tests have been conducted to show that the changes from

stage to stage of sleep are due to chemical signals that obey some necessary body rhythm. When the chemical norepine-phrin is injected into a human or an animal during one of the other stages of sleep, the subject shifts immediately into REM sleep. This leaves little doubt that chemistry is responsible for the onset as well as the duration of each stage of sleep. Tests have been conducted on cats to show that when norepinephrine is introduced into the cat's brain, even when the cat is playing with a mouse, the cat will lie down immediately and go into the dream stage of sleep. The action of norepinephrin in producing the dream stage of sleep is hindered or blocked entirely by the use of sleeping pills.

During the REM stage, the thought process seems to be work-ing very hard. The conclusion of scientific studies is that, during the REM stage, various emotional adjustments take place and new information is put in its proper storage place. The things that are placed in storage are the images and symbols with which we remember and think. During stressful periods a person's REM stage of sleep increases in length. When a stroke has destroyed part of the speech vocabulary, strenuous effort is used to learn words again and the REM period increases.

Infant learning in the first months is on a vast scale, coping with all the body processes; countless new sights, sounds, mo-tions and feelings which flood the brain. This multitude of new signals coming to the infant's brain require long periods of REM sleep to digest the new material.

An infant sleeps around sixteen to eighteen hours a day; half is in REM sleep. Premature infants may have almost one hundred percent REM sleep. The amount of time a child spends in REM sleep remains high during the first six years when there is a stupendous absorption of new material. It is also the period when the brain triples in size. Further brain growth is slow until the age of twelve when the proportions of time spent in REM sleep out of the total amount of sleep remain steady for many years. REM sleep declines very slowly with age. In the very old, stage four sleep may almost cease, but the REM stage remains relatively unchanged.

During REM sleep, dreams do not contain the emotions and

attitudes that conscious thought contains. The emotional level displayed in the dreams is more simple and primitive than when we are awake. The higher levels of judgment appear to be cut off during sleep. Dreams ordinarily do not contain noise, although sometimes there is auditory recall. A small percentage of dreams contain color. If any dream content can be recalled when awakening from the other three stages of sleep, it is only a flash of a scene. During REM sleep, dreams are movie-like, with the scene racing along as if seen from a moving dreamer. The brain demands the occurrence of this process and becomes frantic if deprived of it.

Sleep deprivation

The first experiments in depriving animals of sleep began in 1894. Experiments on persons began in 1896. Tests were made of persons who went to bed but were directed not to go to sleep. It was found that it was possible for a person to stay awake the whole first night with effort, but it was impossible for him to stay awake during the second night or any successive nights. Some kind of physical activity is needed in order to stay awake during the night. The attempt to take lecture notes after the first sleepless night is difficult. After the second night it is not successful. It was found that after sixty-five hours of wakefulness, a person cannot get any more sleepy.

Sleep loss is felt in a series of steps in the amount of alertness or drowsiness rather than a steady progression of weariness. Even forty—eight hours without sleep makes a person unable to maintain a focus of attention. His memory of what has just occurred is faulty. Periods of fantasy involuntarily occupy his attention. This state of reverie may actually be a type of light sleep with the eyes open.

There are two classic examples reported of voluntary sleep deprivation for publicity. In 1959 Peter Trip, a New York music record radio announcer, stayed out of bed, claiming wakefulness for over 200 hours. His behavior was observed during most of this time. He suffered slurred speech, hallucinations and paranoiac suspicions of even his most trusted supporters. Each day he was able to work up his attention for short bursts of rational concentration and speech. Whether he could sleep on his feet with his eyes open was not determined.

In 1965 Randy Gardner, a seventeen year old from San Diego stayed up for 264 hours. He was monitored at all times. It was almost impossible to keep him awake at night. He had to be kept in motion, but even then it was thought that he had frequent micro-sleeps. His monitors and supporters had difficulty keeping his eyes open. In both of these cases the individuals began to function after about eighteen hours of sleep. They suffered weariness for over two weeks.

Nighttime acrobatics

Does anyone sleep like a log? No. You change your position at least forty times. Your subconscious mind is guarding you to keep your muscles and joints from getting stiff, and your blood supply moving to all parts of your body. Without knowing it, you may scratch, rub, twitch, jerk, kick, make faces, mutter gibberish and turn over. You adjust the covers to fit the temperature, avoid rolling out of bed, and turn off the alarm without knowing it. You may give yourself directions to awaken at a particular time. With practice you will be more and more accurate in obeying your self-direction. The watchful part of your brain remains aware at all times.

Learning while you sleep

At one time great hopes arose that you could learn from recordings played to you while you were asleep. Efforts have been made, in the western world and in Russia, to find a way to accomplish learning during sleep. All tests so far show that the hopes for sleep learning are in vain. If sleep learning can occur, it happens only during the threshold period of wakefulness just before the beginning of stage one of sleep, as you are floating down the slope of awareness toward that second when the senses turn off into sleep. When sleep arrives the awareness of sound cuts off, so that the brain is free from the myriad jumble of signals coming to it from the outside.

A Sleep Cycle

(Ninety minutes)

STAGE	BRAIN WAVE	FEELINGS	BODY CHANGES
Threshold	Even and steady, 9 to 15 waves per second.	Relaxed, wandering thoughts. Awareness decreasing. Senses dulled. May twitch.	Body functions, muscle tension decreasing.
I	Size smaller, slower.	Awaken easily. Will not believe having slept.	Gradual decrease in all body processes.
II	Larger, slower occasional bursts.	Sound easily awakens, but eyes cannot see.	Decrease: pulse, breathing, blood pressure, metabolism, temperature, secretions. Eyes may roll.
III	One per second but five times as big as in I.	More difficult to awaken.	All the above body processes continue decreasing.
IV	Large, slow, wandering, uneven.	Very difficult to awaken.	Lowest level of body processes.
REM	Small, irregular. Big bursts.	Very difficult to awaken. Elaborate dreams.	Eyes dart about. Muscles limp. Blood pressure, breathing, pulse way up and down.

Chapter II

GET THE JUNGLE
OUT OF YOUR SYSTEM

If you can get the jungle out of your day, it will help you to gain control over your sleep. The human body is a highly evolved complex organism that responds to its environment in the world today as it has been doing during the primitive conditions of the evolutionary process. The instinctive protective responses have not changed from those developed during the countless ages of prehistory. Survival of the individual during that long period depended on sensing and reacting to danger quickly and successfully. Chemically the brain is illiterate, not recognizing verbal niceties of civilized life. It recognizes only two signals; danger and calm.

When the danger signal to the brain warned of some emergency, the body and the brain prevented sleep. Only when the brain was receiving the no danger signal, could it give commands for sleep to occur. Chemical actions in the brain and body on the signal of danger fire up the whole organism for the test of self-preservation. On the signal for calm, the body slows down again for self renewal and sleep.

17

Facing attack and fear of death

The brain, in its primitive intelligence, recognized danger as overwhelmingly important because the failure to react to danger quickly and successfully was death. Modern human behavior was formed during the millenniums of time by trial and error. Those brains, which did not interpret danger correctly, did not survive to continue their misinterpretation in later generations. In primitive existence, however, the signal to the brain for danger, together with the combat ready status of all the muscles, nerves and organs of the body, was not up constantly. Usually a threat lasted seconds, minutes or at most, hours. In between there was napping and calm activity. Ideally the spurt of activity throughout the body upon sudden danger was as temporary as the pictures of zebras on the African plain show. A small herd of zebras will answer the threat of a charging lion by running a short distance beyond the charging distance of any lion in sight, but within five minutes, all of the zebras have ended their excitement by peacefully grazing again.

Chemical reactions produced by alarm

Whether the signal for alarm took place during the past millenniums of primitive existence or is taking place today, the brain gives the same commands to the body. The pituitary gland gives orders to the hypothalamus and through the body to other glands. The heart is speeded up, breathing becomes deeper, sweat gland production increases especially on the palms of the hands and in the armpits. The digestive organs are ordered to slow down or stop, the salivary glands to dry up, more white blood corpuscles are released to fight injury, more adrenalin is secreted into the blood to increase muscle capability, the pupils of the eyes dilate, the hearing is sharpened, the liver discharges sugar into the blood, the spleen releases more red blood corpuscles and the small blood vessels constrict in the fingers and toes while increasing the flow of blood to the head.

Further manifestations of reaction to the alarm signal is the tensing of the muscles around the eyes, the forehead and brow, the face, the neck, the throat, the jaw, the mouth and the tongue.

Even the scalp becomes tighter. In some animals this causes the fur to stand out. The chest is tightened and the esophagus constricts to feel like a lump in the throat. The leg muscles are tightened and aquiver and the hands and feet move.

When the signal of alarm sets off all the chemistry and commands enumerated, the tension might be terminated by heavy physical activity of combat or flight. Such physical activity would dissipate much or all of the tension when the alarm signals stopped coming from the brain. There was a point and a good reason for the enormous mobilization of body resources for self-preservation.

Chemical reactions from modern alarms

In our modern life all the manifestations detailed in the last section are with us with a vengeance. The brain interprets the threats to our work life, to our home life, to our social life, to our comforts and to our self image as if they were threats to our life. The brain gives the same orders to the whole human organism as those in primitive life. The brain recognizes only the alarm, not whether it is caused by a wild beast, a job competitor or highway traffic. Instead of the alarm being over in seconds, minutes or hours, we pointlessly allow the alarm to go on for weeks, months and years. Two side effects from this continuous chemical alarm are the increased desire for starches and a decrease in digestive activity which causes the food consumed to ferment, producing indigestion.

Perpetual alarm

If we allow it, the result of perpetual tension will produce irritation, quarrelsomeness, aggression and depression. It aggravates marriage relations, sexual relations, friendship and work relations. Internally it produces stomach ulcers, constipation and other intestinal disorders; psychosomatic hayfever and asthma, skin blemishes, eruptions and headaches. Illnesses last longer and develop more easily. Wounds take longer to heal. Laughter is inhibited.

It has been demonstrated that when a mouse is kept in a cage next to a cage with a cat in it, the mouse will rapidly age from a state of alarm and tension. In a few days it will die. The chemistry acting in the body of the mouse is similar, in a lesser degree, to the chemistry acting on our own bodies when we are in a constant state of apprehension.

Changes evident in the body due to the existence of modern tension are many. Besides those affecting the heart, the blood vessels and the digestive tract, they include enlarged adrenal glands, shrunken lymph nodes and thyroid gland, high blood sugar and high blood pressure.

Psychosomatic illnesses

The term, phychosomatic illness, relates to conditions that occur because of the individual constantly signalling to the brain that the body needs to be in a combat ready status.

One of the earlier writers on the subject, Dr. John A. Schindler of the Monroe Clinic, described such conditions as "emotionally induced illness." He said that over fifty percent of all those seeking medical help had self-inflicted, emotionally induced illness. The doctor cannot cure such an illness with medicine. Dr. Schindler made a chart of the percentage of sufferers of common illnesses that are caused by emotionally induced actions. Some of them went up to ninety-nine percent. Constipation was at seventy percent, intestinal, ulcer and gall bladder pain at fifty percent, neck pains at seventy-five percent and throat pain at ninety percent. Present day estimates are much higher. Schindler also said of the approximately one thousand diseases which human beings can have, emotionally induced illness is more common than all the other 999 added together.

A present day doctor estimated that two-thirds of all people die of emotionally induced illness. This is not because our bodies are used up by ordinary wear and tear, but because the constant self-induced state of alarm sooner or later wrecks a part of the body that is essential for survival. The effect of emotionally induced illness on an individual gets worse year by year. Dr. Schindler theorized that the brain interprets anything that offends us as a reason to set up the alarm status.

The self-inflicted emotionally caused illness affects even those few who have escaped having it. It decreases the standard of living of the nation by poor health on and off the job and removes many from the productive process when they have reached their peak economic value. It increases the cost of accident, health and auto insurance.

Dr. Schindler summarized the emotions that he believed cause tension and stress. He named anxiety, fear, apprehension, discouragement, disappointment, frustration, anger and hate. Some other causes were impatience, fear of failure, futility, despair, grief, concern and worry and aggression. Most people do not die of old age, but die of emotionally induced illness that is brought on by mistaking the modern pressures of living as a threat to life under primitive conditions.

Evidences of internal stress

The conditions of emotional stress in your daily life affect the speed with which you can learn to control your sleep. Research has left no doubt that natural sleep is affected by the mental, emotional and stressful activity of the day. Electroencephalograms show that anxiety can still be present in the form of tension even after enough relaxation has developed to permit sleep. The voluntary and involuntary muscles in their tension, aching and stiffness are a mirror of what is going on inside the body. The many books on tension claim that it takes more lives than any other illness. The failure to achieve relaxation is one of the prime causes of death.

Tension squanders your energy, which is demonstrated in an obvious way, when you exert ten times the needed muscles to hold a pencil, a glass or the steering wheel of an auto. Other overexertions are hidden from you. The heavy smoker, the over-drinker and the over-eater are trying to obtain relief from tension.

Physical movements giving signs of tension or emotionally induced illness are foot tapping, winding the foot around chair legs, crossing and uncrossing the legs, shuffling the feet, twisting or tapping the fingers, picking, scratching, lip chewing, nail biting, tooth grinding, head scratching, sighing, hyperventilating, belching, face tics, muttering, talking to one's self in traffic, pencil chewing and door slamming. You are usually unaware of your tensions because most of them are beneath the level of awareness, unfelt but acting upon you.

Under modern day conditions of living, the great majority of the population has body conditions similar to a modified state of shock.

The attitude of tension and anxiety is so widespread that it is the standard instead of the abnormal behavior. Neurotic behavior is so general that it is considered normal.

Some authorities have estimated that the muscles and organs of over thirty percent of American adults go into the jungle combat state of tension almost immediately upon awakening. They remain in it until sleep comes over them again. The sleep of such persons is slow in coming. It is less restful because of the residual tension that lasts all night and you are more likely to wake during the night.

Experiments have shown that the muscles and organs react to the memory of threats to your interests as well as to the original experiencing of the threat. A laboratory example shows that repeated blows to the forearm cause a reaction from the automatic nervous system which changes the flow of blood into the forearm. A feigned blow to the forearm will cause the automatic nervous system to make the same change in the flow of blood as the real blow did. Memory of anger will produce physiological changes to the muscles and organs closely resembling the changes caused by the original anger. The repeated self-injury by constant false alarms to the nervous system is not only detrimental to well-being during the day, but the effects are cumulative, becoming greater with each passing year.

Our objective is to reduce the effects of the constant false alarm status in the body and brain by calming the disturbances within us through the means of self-training for sleep. Eventually one or more of the sleep techniques will enable us to terminate the emotional pressure and irritation of our organism and restore some kind of harmony between our body and our activities. All the surveys show that a result of self-training for sleep is an increase in the productivity and effectiveness of each hour. It also increases the number of hours of productivity each day.

Over ninety-nine percent of those questioned, who have adopted a plan of self-training for sleep, claim that they are calmer, more secure and tolerate problems better. Nearly all the training is done mentally. Lest this kind of training seem unusual to you, musicians improve their performance by playing pieces in their minds. Athletes rehearse events by going through them mentally with improved results.

Doctors often tell their patients to become as informed as possible about their own afflictions. The self-training sleep techniques offered should make you a specialist on your own sleep problem.

1965 Stress Evaluation Table of Dr. T. H. Holmes related in weight to anxiety and vigilance interference with setting the stage for good sleep.

Event	*Point Value*
Death of Spouse	100
Divorce	73
Marital Separation	65
Jail Term	63
Death of close family member	63
Personal injury or illness	53
Getting married	50
Fired at work	47
Reconciliation with mate	45
Retirement	45
Changed health in family member	44
Pregnancy	40
Sex difficulties	39
Gaining a new family member	39
Business readjustment	39
Change in financial status	38
Death of a close friend	37
Change to a different line of work	36
Increase in arguments with mate	35
Mortgage over $10,000.00	31

Foreclosure of mortgage or loan 30
Change in work responsibility 29
Child leaving home 29
Trouble with in-laws 29
Outstanding personal achievement 28
Mate begins or ends work 26
Change in living conditions 25
Revision of personal habits 24
Trouble with boss 23
Changed work hours or conditions 20
Change in residence 20
Change in schools 20
Change in recreation 20
Change in church activities 19
Change in social activities 18
Mortgage or loan under $10,000.00 16
Changed number of family meetings 16
Change in sleeping habits 16
Change in eating habits 15
Vacation 13
Christmas 12
Minor violation of law 11

Chapter III

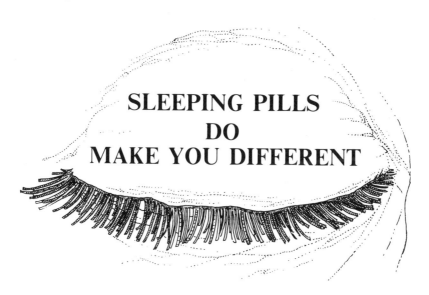

SLEEPING PILLS DO MAKE YOU DIFFERENT

The desire for the benefits of sleep and relaxation has been so great that individuals have turned to the use of drugs in enormous numbers. The percentage of sleeping pills prescribed has increased each year; the total amount five times as many over a twelve year period. The total market cost of sleeping pills runs into the billions of dollars each year. Heroin and morphine products were about all you could get for sleep for a long time. Drug addiction was so certain and its horrors so terrible, that when barbiturates were discovered in 1903, doctors were pleased and hopeful about the new alternative.

It took many years before the knowledge slowly developed that withdrawal from barbiturate addiction could be even worse than withdrawal from heroin and morphine. It was found that barbiturates could destroy your personality and ability more seriously than heroin and morphine. New hopes arose again in the 1950's when tranquilizers were developed. Other drugs have been introduced in the search for harmless sleep inducers, but up to this time, all of them have failed to produce normal sleep and all have harmful side effects.

All of our actions and reactions are chemical in nature. Excitement and depression are the result of chemical actions within us. The chemical action on the brain from sleeping pills had to interfere with natural chemical actions already going on in the brain and body.

How sleeping pills act upon you

The purpose of sleeping pills is to alter the brain chemically. There are many variations of the formulas for barbiturates produced by the different drug companies, but the most frequently prescribed barbiturates are phenobarbital, seconal, amytal and nembutal. They are absorbed into the white matter of the brain and into the nerves. Some varieties will be absorbed in as little as ten or fifteen minutes. Some take as long as an hour to attack the brain. Disappearance of the barbiturate from the body takes up to two weeks. When a prescribed dosage is taken each night, the level of accumulation can increase night by night until the level is much higher than a single dose. The action of tranquilizers and other sleeping compounds is accomplished by causing the same change upon the brain and nervous system. A similar accumulation also occurs.

Effect of sleeping pills on the quality of sleep

Some individuals believe that legal drugs are safe and illegal drugs are dangerous. There are no grounds for considering legal drugs safe. The electroencephalogram records from the sleep laboratories show that the single stage of sleep that is changed by sleeping pills is the REM dream stage. As cited in the last chapter, many studies have shown that the Rem stage of sleep is required for normal sleep and mental health. Deprivation of such sleep, with or without drugs, causes loss of efficiency, vitality and emotional stability. Because one of the effects of sleeping pills is to reduce or prevent REM stage of sleep, the prolonged use of them results in a trance-like state instead of sleep. After withdrawal from sleeping pills the unnatural sleep quality may continue for as long as two months.

Changed behavior with use of sleeping pills

The use of a gram or more of barbiturates will cause an individual's speech to slur, his gait to appear to be staggering and will cause a general state of mental confusion. The barbiturate addict tends to neglect his appearance. His friends will notice the changes. He loses interest in his job and eventually his job is lost. His clarity of mind is rare. His judgment becomes erratic and poor. His ambition and concern for his self-interests and self-protection declines.

Other changes include a reduction in imagination and ability to learn. The intellectual activity portion of the brain is affected for a lasting period. Memory is impaired for eight hours or more after taking a barbiturate, because of the lingering effect of partial paralysis of the nerve and brain cells. The results of IQ tests decline and enthusiasm dissipates.

Side effects that are known

Variable conditions affecting each person's reaction to sleeping pills are many. There are individual differences in the heredity of each of us. We are different in chemical make-up and reaction. Body size makes a difference. Illness or the lack of illness may change susceptibility greatly. The older you are, the slower your body expels the drug. An aged person on an unchanged nightly dosage accumulates much higher levels of the drug in his body than a younger person.

One of the first side effects noticed by the beginning drug user is an increase in constipation. Women, with a different body chemistry than men, are more sensitive to sleeping pills.

Thalidomide was a sleeping pill that deformed the development of fetuses. The fetus usually lacked fingers, toes, arms or legs. Since the 1960's there has been a suspicion that at least some sleeping pills used by pregnant women were the cause of cataracts in the eyes of infants. On July 22, 1976, the Federal Drug Administration published a warning stating that tranquilizers may cause birth defects when used by pregnant women. Most of the damage is caused in the first two weeks of pregnancy. Unfortunately the existence of pregnancy is not known in the first two weeks, so a woman cannot protect her fetus by discontinuing use of tranquilizers as soon as she learns of the pregnancy. The damage is probably already done and is irreversible.

Other factors related to sleeping pills

Food interacts with sleeping pills, increasing or decreasing their effect. Exposure to insecticides may cause sleeping pills to have an intensified effect, even long after exposure to the insecticide. Some people are agitated by the presence of sleeping pills in the system. Some users wake up with intense shoulder and neck pain from barbiturates.

A flare-up of allergies can occur. For persons who have a metabolic disease called porphyria, a barbiturate can cause a reaction producing paralysis or death. Interaction between sleeping pills is a vast, unexplored unknown. Some persons may be taking as many as a dozen kinds of pills at one time. One drug can amplify the effect of another, even to the extent of producing convulsions. In one reported instance, the effect of sleeping pills interacting with some other pills caused a mistaken diagnosis of insanity. The person was committed to a mental institution before the effect of the interacting drugs wore off.

Surprise reactions

Some persons suddenly develop an extreme sensitivity to sleeping pills. They become disabled by what would otherwise have little effect. Sometimes when the use of a barbiturate is discontinued, upon resumption of use an extreme susceptibility develops. Those on heavy dosages of sleeping pills may develop a skin rash, blurred vision and dizziness. Non-prescription drugs containing scopalamine taken in excess will cause scopalamine poisoning that leads to hallucinations, convulsions and coma.

Some heart attacks are caused by the strains that result when a user of barbiturates consumes alcohol, especially before going to bed. For those individuals who have had a heart attack or a stroke, barbiturates will block the effect of any anti-coagulant they might take.

Older persons who were thought to have had brain damage from hardening of the arteries and senile dementia had, instead, been using sleeping pills for so many years that they became trance-like. When these persons withdrew from sleeping pills, some became as alert as ever.

Sleeping pills cause insomnia

Because your body's tolerance of any kind of sleeping pill soon rises to the level of dosage you are taking, it is only ten days until the pills yield no sleep inducement to you at all, except by the placebo effect.

A placebo is a pill prescribed by a physician which you are told will have a beneficial effect, but is really nothing but sugar. Experience shows that for some kinds of pills, as high as seventy percent of those receiving the placebo, will get the benefit they expect because of the power of suggestion.

Even though sleeping pills taken on a fixed dosage no longer induce sleep, your sleep is restless and unnatural. The pills interfere with the quality and onset of REM dream sleep. This condition produces the insomnia that the pills are supposed to prevent. Frequent awakenings will continue until the dosage is increased or discontinued.

If you take sleeping pills intermittently, the first night or nights after the intermittent use will be uneasy, for the brain tries to catch up on the REM dream stage. This REM period may be frenzied enough to awaken you, or to give you a nightmare. Unfortunately, it is a human tendency to ignore distress signals from the body and brain, blaming them on other things.

Highway traffic toll and pills

One study estimates that one out of twelve auto drivers on the highway are under the influence of sleeping pills or amphetamines. Drug users are involved in as many as 15,000 traffic deaths per year. The study indicates that drug users have ten times as many traffic accidents as do non-users. Some of these users stop for an alcoholic drink, becoming a still greater traffic hazard. Because blood tests after traffic accidents are for alcohol only, no records are kept of the presence of drugs in drivers. After an airplane crash there is a test made for drugs in the blood of flight personnel. Should not a similar test be given drivers involved in accidents? Highway deaths due to drug use may be as large as those attributable to the use of alcohol.

Accidental death

Because of the confused, trance-like state a barbiturate user is in after taking his dosage, he is in constant danger of unknowingly taking another dose without remembering that he has taken the first dose. In fact experience shows that the second dose is taken without judgment and may be much larger than a single dosage. Such a user may never wake up to find out that he has taken an overdose. Between this kind of accident and all other drug related fatalities, one authority estimates that there are 40,000 drug related deaths per year in the United States. It was previously stated that 15,000 was the portion attributable to the highway. Part of these are related to the use of amphetamines. These numbers do not include deaths due to the use of alcohol.

Alcohol and barbiturates

Of all drug addictions, the use of alcohol is the principal one, dominating the behavior of from ten to thirty-five million Americans. As a drug, the effect of alcohol on the quality of sleep closely resembles that of sleeping pills. It deprives sleep of the REM dream stage.

Both drugs have a paralyzing effect on the nervous system and the brain which gives the orders for body functions. Alcohol is a pure fuel, which the body defends itself against by oxidizing it. The action of a barbiturate is to block the process of oxidation.

The result is a state of unconsciousness that destroys the brain's control over body functions. The temperature slowly falls and, at some point, breathing stops.

Withdrawal

Even light users of sleeping pills have a problem with withdrawal. The first night of withdrawal is an uneasy one as the brain tries to catch up on the lost amount of REM sleep. REM stage is a frenzied time for the brain under normal circumstances and becomes more so during withdrawal. Very often a person gives up after the first rude awakening from a disturbing dream, goes to the medicine cabinet and resumes taking sleeping pills. The feeling of being restless, or failure to sleep frightens the withdrawer. For light users of sleeping pills making an attempt to withdraw, it is better to shave off a little from the dosage each night for a period of several weeks.

Heavy users of sleeping pills who try to withdraw have such violent and frightening nightmares, that most give up after a few efforts. Sudden withdrawal from heavy use causes days of apprehension, dehydration, rapid pulse, fast over breathing, weakness, hallucinations and even convulsions. The nights are the same, plus insomnia. Painless withdrawal may take as long as eighteen months. It is achieved by a very gradual reduction in dosage.

The withdrawal and recovery from the heavy use of tranquilizers is shorter than withdrawal from barbiturates. For many persons the withdrawal from barbiturates is so long that the resolve may be lost along the way. For many persons, success requires medical supervision.

Double abuse

Stay-awake pills or amphetamines have health disadvantages similar to those of sleeping pills. Amphetamines also accomplish their effect by changing the chemistry of the brain. The double abuse comes when the consumer of sleeping pills awakens in a groggy state. He believes he has to take amphetamines in order to get through the day. Office workers may use amphetamines to stay awake. Students may use them the night before examinations. We have an authoritative estimate that half of the total amphetamine production is obtained without the use of prescriptions. Ninety percent of the non-prescription use is by long haul truck drivers. Other names given to the pills are pep pills, speed pills, happy pills and uppers.

The cells of the body rapidly develop a tolerance for amphetamines. Larger and larger dosages are required in order to get the same effect as with the first pill. With amphetamines, when the dosage gets high enough, the user develops apprehension, suspicion, hostility and hallucinations.

Amphetamines give the user a false belief that he is not tired, but the stay-awake pills do not decrease fatigue in any way. They do mislead the brain so that it cannot protect the body from the fatigue that is actually there. The body is just as tired as if the stay-awake pills had not been taken. An individual's reaction time and accuracy of physical and mental judgment decline as rapidly as if the pills had not been taken. High dosages of stay-awake pills can make a vehicle driver see things in the vehicle and on the highway that are not there; such as snakes, fixed and moving objects and other people. When such hallucinations are present, the chances for a safe trip are close to zero.

Chapter IV

GATEWAYS
TO APPROACH
SLEEP TECHNIQUE

Success in learning sleep techniques will be easier and quicker if you start with an adequate background of information. Most of us need to remove some myths surrounding sleep and learn some facts that will help us.

Most of us look upon sleep as a separate phase of existence, independent of the rest of our lives. Such is not the case. As far as the body and the brain are concerned, sleep is a continuation of the activities of the day. Living a good day will help to produce good sleep. Often a poor day will result in poor sleep. The body does not have two lives, one awake and one asleep. Both phases are one continuous life responding to many internal rhythms and a myriad jumble of external influences. Part of our technique will be to turn these rhythms and influences to our advantage in order to control sleep.

Insomnia

A Gallup poll reported that fifty−two percent of Americans have insomnia. It is an affliction recorded as far back as the beginning of history. Most of us have experienced insomnia when we were in a different location or changing the hour of going to bed. It occurs from worry, anxiety, fear, illness or depression.

Complaints about insomnia are divided into four classes: (1), those about long delays in getting to sleep, (2), awakening during the night with difficulty in getting back to sleep, (3), awakening early in the morning and not getting back to sleep, (4), sleeplessness all night long. If you awaken early in the morning without the ability to get back to sleep, you may have had all the sleep you require. Your body clock is telling you that the night is over for you.

Occasional disturbed sleep will not destroy your health physically or mentally, particularly if you can average enough sleep per week. During World War II, residents of some cities had to sleep sporadically because of bombing. Records indicate that the interruptions produced no increase in mental problems. If your only concern about sleep is the occasional loss of a small amount, you may not need to worry. The fear of not being able to go to sleep, especially before days of greater importance, contributes to sleeplessness.

Internal rhythms influence sleep

The body's need for sleep is not entirely related to daylight and darkness. You have twenty-four hour internal rhythms that make you feel the need for sleep. For most of us this biological timing device lets us know by a slowing of body functions; lower temperature, blood pressure, metabolism, cell count; decreasing muscle tension and chemical secretions. For nearly everyone, this cycle reaches a low point sometime between two o'clock and five o'clock in the morning. This explains why night workers have sleep problems and are most tired in the early morning hours.

All night workers who regularly rotate from day to night shifts make some adjustments to the body rhythms during the period of a week, but they cannot overcome the early morning low that affects us all. Night personnel have to recognize these factors as a cause of inefficient production. Studies show that it takes at least two weeks to adjust to night work and day sleeping. Sleeping in the daytime causes the REM stage of sleep to occur sooner. During the two week adjustment, the individual is certain to be listless. When the change is made back to day work and night sleeping, no adjustment is necessary. The body makes the change almost automatically.

Studies made of those who live in the Arctic, with periods of almost twenty-four hours of light and dark, prove that they maintain the same twenty-four hour body rhythms as the rest of us. Experiments where sleep scientists lived in dark caves showed some adjustments to the body rhythms, but the conclusion was that changes are very slow.

The speed of air travel across time zones creates problems for the traveler because his body clock shifts slowly to the new time zone. Athletes who have crossed time zones to Europe, immediately before competing, have found that their performance might come at the time their body clock is trying to tell them they should be asleep. Businessmen and diplomats have had to learn to time their appointments to obey their sleep rhythms. They will not be at their best until jet lag has worn off.

It may be that your personal body clock is set for sleeping at an earlier or later hour than the time you try to go to sleep. Most persons have experimented to find the best hour for them. It is good practice to be ready to get into bed nearly a half an hour before your best hour for going to sleep.

Those, whose rhythm of when to sleep and when to be awake, makes them slow to awaken are inattentive at school in the morning, but are likely to be alert in the afternoon. Some persons are at their peak in the morning, some in the afternoon and a few are at their peak in the evening. It is better to cooperate with your body rhythm than to oppose it.

The rhythms of the body and brain are so pervasive that any interruption of their regularity causes us to get out of kilter with ourselves. This is one of the reasons it is important to select and keep a regular hour for going to bed. This will assure maximum synchronization with the natural rhythms of the body.

The ninety minute cycle

We first met the ninety minute cycle when we looked at the stages of sleep which average ninety minutes in length all through the night. The theory has been tested that the ninety minute cycle continues all through the day. This is verified in tests of subjects kept in isolation or in the dark.

The ninety minute rhythm relates to the accumulation and discharge of basic drives. These drives are sleep, hunger, sex and aggression. They all come from the same part of the brain stem.

An experiment observing individuals kept in isolation showed that there was a ninety minute eating cycle. Every ninety minutes a subject wanted to put something in his mouth; food, drink or a cigarette. Further experiments show that the ninety minute cycle becomes shorter during the day, as it does during the night, when an individual is under emotional stress. A person under stress may become overweight as his rhythmic urge to eat comes oftener.

You have probably experienced this rhythm on the evening of a long social engagement, when you have sensed a time of extreme drowsiness and wished you could go to sleep. Later when you got home the drowsiness was gone and you felt wide awake. It is probable that sleep will not come easily until ninety minutes from the point when you were last at the peak of drowsiness.

The records show that the life-long shape and length of the ninety minute cycle is affected by anxiety, illness, drugs and brain damage. When you decrease stress, anger and anxiety, you improve the quality of your sleep. Then you can decrease the quantity of sleep you need.

False insomnia

Sleep laboratory records have repeatedly proved that persons who believed they were awake nearly all night slept more than they realized. The encephalogram record proves that they were going through the different stages of sleep with regularity. They had really been asleep when they claimed they were awake. Such persons either dreamed that they were awake during the night, or only waking time was remembered. In the hospital, patients often claim that they could not sleep all night, but the duty nurse knows that the patient snored and gave all the evidence of sound sleep.

There are a few persons who intentionally cut down on the amount they sleep. Some do so because they believe they are getting enough, some because they begrudge sleep time they are taking from another activity. A very few carry a fear of sleep from early in life. A small number of persons feel mistreated by life and take it out on the world by making a plea for sympathy by claiming insomnia. Depriving yourself of your required amount of sleep is as harmful as loss of sleep from any other cause.

How much sleep do you need?

It is not possible to judge your own requirements of sleep by comparing your characteristics with anyone else's. Even between members of the same family, the differences in the ease of going to sleep, or in the amount of sleep required varies, just as appetite varies. You have to make the judgment of your requirements for yourself.

It is a myth that every adult needs eight hours of sleep. Some need nine, and some need six. The range can be even greater. One person has been documented at four hours of sleep regularly. Two persons have been checked out at a little over three hours of sleep per night. Naps must be included in sleep time. Seven hours or a little more is the usual amount. Some people doze at their desks or before the TV. It all counts. Many night workers sleep twice a day; once soon after getting home, and the second time just before going to work.

Does it matter when we sleep? If it is your habitual time and fits your own body rhythms, the answer is no. Those who take naps whenever possible usually go to sleep more easily at night. In general, acceptance of your sleeping habits and rituals is helpful. Pregnancy may change those habits because more sleep is then required, sometimes as much as two hours.

You cannot store up extra sleep. For very small losses of sleep, you cannot sleep more in order to catch up. Usually all that is needed to catch up is a regular night's sleep. However, laboratory records show that the quality of sleep displayed on the encephalograms does not return to normal range for each individual until the third night after the sleep loss. Sleep loss does change the quality of sleep the first night after the loss.

We cannot expect to go to sleep easily every night. Good

sleepers are successful in quickly going to sleep only about ninety percent of the time. Going to sleep and waking up are both gradual events, each taking about a half hour for the process in the body and brain to take place. Responsible mental activity should not be expected or planned until more than a half hour after awakening. It is worthwhile to get up slowly while the body processes change their level of activity to daytime efficiency. Few individuals wake up bright and alert. Some sleep experts advise smiling during the awakening, instead of groaning, on the grounds that either one will shape the whole day.

Other factors in the amount of sleep needed

Experience shows that older people need just as long a sleep period per day as younger people, but the quality of their sleep is different. Their sleep is interrupted more often with periods of wakefulness. Also they go to sleep less quickly. Deep sleep of stage four takes up to two hours per night in younger persons, but declines in amount in the older persons until it is almost zero in the very elderly.

Women have twice as much as insomnia as men. Women do not sleep as deeply as men on the average and awaken more easily than men.

What does loss of sleep do to you?

Sleep experiments show that on the day following the loss of sleep, work efficiency, reaction time and memory are adversely affected. Tiny naps may occur with the eyes open or shut. The person may not be aware of them. Accidents are more likely to occur at home, at work and on the highway. An Oklahoma study estimated that twenty—two percent of accidents on the highway involved sleepy drivers. A California study showed nineteen percent of single car accidents involved drivers asleep or sleepy. Not all of these drivers may have lost sleep before driving. There is a percentage of drivers who are in a type of trance during night driving. Tests have been devised to show if night driving conditions decrease the level of consciousness of drivers. Some drivers cannot remain awake more than ten minutes after starting to drive at night. Auto accident reports generally contain no record of the hours of sleep of the drivers. In aviation accident reports, the Civil Aeronautics Board requires a record of the amount of sleep during the previous twenty–four hours of each member of the crew. Often the records reveal little sleep during the twenty–four hour period.

A night's loss of sleep does not decrease muscular strength. Noticeable behavioral changes appear from sleep deprivation, such as irritability, hostility, depression and lack of energy. Lack of sleep is associated with stomach ulcers. Some of the effects of fatigue can be overcome by continual physical activity or by drinking coffee and cola.

Naps are a practical method of making up for lost sleep. Daytime naps have a different shape of brain wave from those of night sleep. Generally morning naps contain as much as one–third of the REM stage of sleep, but afternoon sleep does not. Deep stage four sleep appears in the afternoon naps but not in the morning. This explains why it is harder to awaken from afternoon naps. You are sleepier after an afternoon nap than after a morning nap.

Long sleepers and short sleepers

An experiment was arranged of two groups of people who answered ads, one group of those who claimed that they always slept less than six hours; the other group who claimed they slept over nine hours a night. The encephalogram records of their sleep showed that the long sleepers were in the dream stage of REM sleep almost twice as long as the short sleepers and spent much more of the night awake. This would indicate that the long sleepers may have been subject to more stress, worry, anxiety and depression. The short sleepers were more free from these concerns. Short sleepers appeared to live by habit. They were busy and relatively free from doubts or reflections. Some attempt was made to generalize about the personality differences of the two groups without reaching a conclusion.

Good sleepers and poor sleepers

A study assembled two groups of people. One group claimed they were good sleepers, the other group claimed they were poor sleepers. From an examination of the encephalogram records made by each of the two groups, the good sleepers went to sleep in an average of seven minutes. The poor sleepers took an average of fifteen minutes. These times were quicker than either class of sleeper believed. Most persons do go to sleep more quickly than they believe they do.

Further differences in the two groups were that the poor sleepers were awake more often. They got an average of forty-five minutes less sleep per night. The poor sleepers had an average higher temperature and a faster pulse before and during sleep. They moved more often while asleep. One theory is that the poor sleepers may be trying to get more sleep than they actually need.

Another study concluded that some poor sleepers were trying to sleep during a part of the twenty—four hour period that was out of phase with their body rhythms of temperature, pulse, drowsiness and other factors. Unfortunately for some of them, they are on a work schedule that requires them to get up earlier or later than suits their body clock. The insomnia complaints of such poor sleepers are real and legitimate.

Turning from side to side during the night is stimulated by the nose. The nose becomes congested on the low side after a time. This gives a signal to the body to alternate sides rather rhythmically. Failure to move from time to time is bad for the circulation, the joints and the fluid in the lungs. Clots can develop from stagnant blood due to failure to move periodically. The muscles eventually become numb because they lack oxygen, food supply and retain waste matter.

A few myths

Being drowsy means more sleep is needed. It could mean the opposite. It might signify boredom, inactivity or some kind of anxiety. It could be the bottom of a body rhythm. Experiment to find your own best length of sleep.

We need sleep that is dreamless. Not true. Sleep containing dream periods is a necessary part of healthy sleep.

Trying hard to get to sleep helps bring sleep. False. Trying harder just pumps more stimulating adrenalin into your blood stream. The relaxed "don't care" attitude helps to invite sleep.

Deep sleep means motionless sleep. Wrong. The muscles, joints, nerves, blood vessels and body fluids all require frequent change of position for normal sleep.

The best sleep is before midnight. Perhaps for some persons. The best sleep has to fit your body cycle when the low point in the level of body activity takes place; usually between two o'clock and five o'clock in the morning.

Lying still means you are relaxed. Not necessarily. You can be lying quietly and motionless and still be aware of many tensions, or have many tense muscles of which you are not aware.

Watching TV rests and recuperates. False. Some of the programs will anger, stimulate or excite during the program and carry over afterwards into bed.

A smoke before bedtime is relaxing. Not likely. Smoking has a stimulating capacity in constricting the capillaries and causing the heart to pump harder.

The following chapters are an exploration of the present day established methods of self training for sleep. The methods have many points of intersection and similarity. You can sample the methods and pick the one that seems to fit you. When you decide which method you are going to follow, persist in following it to success. Make it a part of your life. The small effort you put forth will produce rewards in installments that will grow, making enormous changes to your advantage. Just undertaking a program of self training makes you feel good. There is no point in wanting something you cannot have, but you can have good sleep.

Chapter V

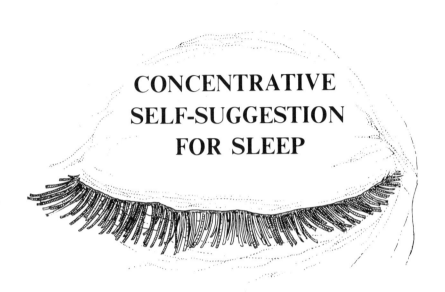

CONCENTRATIVE SELF-SUGGESTION FOR SLEEP

This method is part of the autogenic training system for sleep. It is a scientifically tested system that uses several fields of knowledge to create a method for improving physical and mental health. It was created under Dr. J.H. Schultz in Germany over a period of many years. Since 1932 it has attracted followers throughout the world. As with any field of knowledge, it has changed to make use of new discoveries. It has had several names since its original one; concentrative relaxation.

Autogenic training has many followers among physicians in Europe, Japan, India and North America. It seeks a cure for the two-thirds or more of bodily illness that are self-inflicted.

Autogenic, meaning self-suggestion, is related to self-hypnosis, but is scientifically developed. It is also related to meditation. The autogenic system is more tangible, more clearly defined and more understandable than either hypnosis or meditation. Most of its teachers are psychiatrists. The contents of the several training lectures have been set out in detail for self-instruction. Followers of the self-suggestion method should have complete faith in achieving success in learning this system. A few persons will succeed the first night. A few especially resistant persons will succeed only after many nights of practice. Doubts about success will delay success. Faith in success will speed it.

For those doing the training exercises for better health and improved use of the mind, the exercises are all done during the day, or one is done during the day and the other before going to sleep. For these persons, two exercises of five minutes are recommended daily. The objective is to influence the body through the mind by the power of suggestion. Once you have set a goal, you will continue to move toward it. If sick thoughts are your goal, a sick body body will evolve. Whatever we cultivate and whatever our thoughts are is what we will be. If we believe we cannot go to sleep, then we cannot. The negative thought is often a type of self-torture. Good goals, faith and hope will heal and will lengthen life.

Autogenic training or concentrative relaxation by self-suggestion was developed to cope with the mental and physical condition of unneeded readiness for combat, which is responsible for over two-thirds of the death rate. Nearly all those who have followed autogenic self-training believe that they have reached psychic health. They believe that events can no longer agitate them.

Self-suggestion is not new to you. You have used it on yourself all your life by saying things to yourself like, "Now I must go to the grocery," "Today I must call the dentist," or "I must stop over-eating." In a sense everything we do is self-suggestion. We give these self-suggestions to ourselves all day long. Your own thought is your master. Whatever you think is what you will become. This thought power you have over yourself can help bring about the conditions for sleep.

Thinking that you will not be able to go to sleep, is a self-suggestion that will come true. Any person who thinks he wants to sleep, will sleep. Unfortunately if he tries to force the coming of sleep, he turns sleep away from him.

A further problem we all have in governing each of our lives is the problem of concentration. In the primitive wilderness, animals and mankind needed to have their attention divided as widely as possible, like a revolving radar screen. But in modern life, successful concentration of the mind brings enormous rewards in two ways. You can attain greater accomplishments if you can concentrate better.

The feverish dancing of the mind on numerous thoughts and ideas causes a high level of electric activity in the brain. This is conducive to chronic physical tension as well as nervous tension. Both these conditions lead to the psychosomatic illnesses afflicting modern mankind. Concentrative self-suggestions that you learn, will increase your capacity for concentration in all other phases of your life. Followers of concentrative self-suggestion methods claim improved health, fewer problems, uninterrupted sleep, greater strength, better digestion and more effective work. Nervous and physical tension is irritating to us, but usually we are not aware of how much our own nervous condition irritates other people.

It is easier for the gentle personality to learn the technique of self-suggestion than for an assertive personality. It is more difficult for the assertive person to lower his self-awareness in order to identify with a different attitude. The restless, overactive or suspicious person also may make slower progress. It is a question of ease of suggestibility. The ability to relax is an enormous accomplishment. Anyone who wishes to attain it must have patience and stamina. Because the method of self-suggestion is based on concentration, it is better not to be under the influence of a full stomach, caffein drinks, alcohol, violent emotions or drugs.

The recommended position is to lie on the back with a small pillow under the head, neck and one under the knees. Eyes are closed, elbows slightly bent, and palms are down. If lying on the back is not comfortable, use your usual position for going to sleep. Your tongue should be loose, the jaws slack and the mouth open. Some advisors prefer the eyes to be focused on emptiness, others advise a focus on the hair line and still others prefer a focus on the end of the nose. Provide for the least noise and light that you can. If you cannot eliminate a noise or irritation, simply say to yourself, "It is unimportant, it is irrelevant." Noise should be reduced to the minimum, however, because the noise level affects the thousands of nerve impulses reaching the brain. The brain remains more active and increases the level of activity of the glands, the muscles and the whole body.

After you have gotten into the proper position, your next objective is to get into the self-suggestive state by saying to yourself, preferably as you exhale in your normal way, "I am pleasantly calm." As you quietly and gently say this, try to move your whole body and mind into a state of pleasant calmness and relaxed concentration. At the beginning, you may say this self-direction to yourself a second or third time as you breathe out.

The second self-direction is to say to yourself on six successive exhalations of normal breathing, "My right arm is getting heavy." Apply complete concentration in a relaxed way making your right arm heavy. The purpose of this self-direction is to relax your muscles and develop a further sense of calm. Left-handed persons may start with the left arm.

While saying the self-direction to yourself, you should continue to concentrate on the objective of what you are saying. Thoughts and ideas will interrupt the concentration in greater number and rapidity than you would have imagined. Each time a new thought interrupts, return your mind back to your self-direction. At the beginning of your training, it may be worthwhile to repeat what you have done by saying again, "I am pleasantly calm," followed by six more times of, "My right arm is becoming heavy," as you breathe out.

A few beginners may sense the right arm becoming heavy during the first night of exercise, but a majority of persons will need several nights of learning the process before a definite feeling of heaviness develops. A small percentage of persons will need several weeks. The feeling of heaviness is a signal to you that the muscles have relaxed.

The third self-direction is also for the right arm. Say to yourself six successive exhalations, "My right arm is becoming warm." Your concentration on this self-direction is an effort to relax the blood vessels of the right arm. You can learn to accomplish this in the same way that the infant learns to use its muscles, by concentration and experiment. When your right arm begins to feel warm, it is a signal to you that you have learned to relax the capillaries and other blood vessels of your right arm. Experiments prove that during this feeling of increased warmth, the weight of the right arm actually does increase appreciably due to the increased amount of blood in it.

After you have learned to increase the warmth of your right arm by your own mental efforts, you can use this ability on other parts of the body. Individuals have used the ability to keep the ears and the feet warm in cold weather. It has also been used to increase the circulation of parts of the body to avoid bed sores.

The development of this new ability is a slow process. Eventually the feeling of control over warmth and heaviness can be caused more rapidly, until you can put the whole process into effect almost immediately by saying simply, "Calm, heavy, warm." These first three steps are preparatory.

The fourth step is no longer preparation, but relates directly to the goal of sleep. First, repeat the introductory self-direction, "I am pleasantly calm." Concentrate for six exhalations on a new self-direction, "I am beginning to go to sleep, I will soon be asleep." As the mind flits off, bring it back to concentration on the self-direction. The success of this procedure will come faster and faster as the weeks pass. If, during the beginning nights, success is not reached at this amount of repetition, you may repeat the last self-direction or repeat the whole procedure.

You can give yourself additional self-directions relating to specific problems in connection with sleep. If noises interfere say, "Noise is irrelevant," during six exhalations. As a general rule, any series of six repetitions should be preceded by the introductory, "I am pleasantly calm."

If your eyes are tired or tense, you can use the self-direction, "My eyes are heavy and calm," as usual with six exhalations. For facial or vocal tension, you can use, "My jaw is heavy, my tongue is heavy." If your intestines seem to be irritated or tense you can use, "My abdomen is pleasantly warm." If your chest and diaphragm feel tense, you can use the self-direction, "My chest and diaphragm are pleasantly warm."

These instructions furnish you with all you need to reach your goal of sleep through concentrative self-suggestion the autogenic training way. The worst mistake beginners make is irregular practice. Just as any desirable behavior can be learned, any undesirable behavior can be unlearned. Any systematically followed practice requires self-discipline. Success will be speeded by spending five minutes each day in any comfortable position following the same technique described above. The objective this time is relaxation instead of sleep. Just five minutes each day will slowly change the characteristics of your day as well as your nights. After practicing the self-suggestion training for a year, the training will not only feel automatic to you, but you will feel that following it is necessary to you.

Eventually you will be able to give orders to your subconscious mind through this method to wake yourself up at any hour. You will learn to go to sleep for a short cat nap on any occasion you desire. You will learn to give other self-suggestions successfully.

All self-directions should be as short as possible and should be positive. It is difficult and improper to execute a negative order in this system. In order to blot out irritations that cannot be removed, take the attitude that they are irrelevant. Frame your self-direction in that way. This method can be used toward annoying persons also. It will cause a surprising improvement in relations between you and the irritating person, because that person will be influenced by your indifference. Resentment against irritations is a form of self-punishment to avoid.

A good phrase of self-direction for all purposes is, "I will be pleasantly calm in any situation." Such autogenic self-training will bring you to bedtime in a healthy mental and emotional state. It will enable you to get the sleep you want when you want it. An added incentive is that you will add materially to the length of your life and the pleasure you get out of it.

Chapter VI

THE KELLY METHOD

A basic part of the Kelly method is an original discovery that explains why the manner of breathing is a major factor in almost all methods of inducing sleep. This factor is the importance of the level of carbon dioxide in the blood. In fact Kelly's discovery may be the reason for the success of all breathing methods in bringing sleep, including Yoga, Zen, meditation and autogenic methods.

Charles P. Kelly was a North Carolina State College professor troubled with sleeplessness. He rejected the stupor and permanent dependence brought on by taking sleeping pills. He tried every method known at the time, including physical fatigue, eye exercises, relaxation systems and every kind of breathing. He was unable to get to sleep with any relaxation technique, but he found that almost any kind of artificial breathing brought drowsiness much faster.

In a thorough manner, Kelly examined all the writings he could locate in the United States over a period of years to find what was known about sleep. He came upon a report of sleep deprivation done in an experiment conducted by Seymour Kety at the University of Pennsylvania. Fifty men were kept awake to measure their body processes by attaching them to electroencephalograms and other equipment. All of the men stayed awake except six. Of all the many conditions being tested, only one condition was different in the six men. That condition was an increased level of carbon dioxide in their blood, or respiratory acidosis, at the time of going to sleep. Carbon dioxide combines with water to form carbonic acid which creates the acidosis. The carbon dioxide is created in the body by the oxidation of food by oxygen. Carbon dioxide is removed from the body through the breath and the way for it to accumulate to a higher level is for less of it to be carried away. Decreased breathing, then, was the cause of the higher level of carbon dioxide.

Medical science had recognized for many years that respiratory acidosis was caused by reduced breathing. Sleeping pills tend to reduce breathing plus attacking the chemistry of the brain. In the Kety report, the question was raised for the first time as to whether carbon dioxide was the cause of going to sleep, and whether it is possible to go to sleep without added respiratory acidosis.

A French team of experimenters in 1913 raised the question as to whether increased acidity in the blood caused the onset of sleep. Other writings revealed that before the discovery of anesthetics, carbon dioxide had been used to put patients to sleep for surgery, sometimes by using their own breath. Carbon dioxide has been used as a depressant for the nervous system in cases of excitability in place of pills. This eliminates the risk of side effects or the development of a tolerance.

Other research indicates that the amount of carbon dioxide in the body affects the activity of the brain. When the muscles are tense or anxiety is present, the rate of breathing is faster. This carries away the carbon dioxide more completely. This also causes increased alkalinity, excitability and less acidosis. Increased acidosis relaxes the capillaries, the tiny blood vessels that connect the artery system with the veins, thus easing the flow of blood and reducing the blood pressure. The conclusion from research reports is that insomnia is caused by lack of respiratory acidosis. The body is extremely sensitive to the balance of alkalinity and acidity. Carbon dioxide is the means by which the balance is maintained. Decreased carbon dioxide retained in the system reduces the rate of breathing. More carbon dioxide in the body increases the rate of breathing.

Although Kelly had already discovered the effect of breathing changes on his own ability to go to sleep, his gleanings from the huge body of sleep literature enabled him to have a scientific basis for establishing the best breathing technique for bringing sleep. He called carbon dioxide produced in the body the natural tranquilizer: the body's own sleep inducing chemical. He considered it superior to any drug. It can't harm the body because if voluntary holding of the breath results in sleep, the involuntary controls of breathing immediately take over reducing the level of carbon dioxide to the amount that the brain directs.

The body does not sense the changes in the percentage of oxygen in the blood unless they are above ten percent. The blood circulates all through the body and back to the heart still containing most of the oxygen it started out with. The muscles take what oxygen they need but the rest continues to circulate. The sensitivity of the brain to an amount of carbon dioxide in the blood is so keen, that a decrease of one-fifth of one percent will change the rate of breathing to a marked degree.

There is no long drawn out training period of breathing yourself into drowsiness and then into sleep by the methods evolved by Kelly. Kelly said that drowsiness and sleep bring on relaxation, not that relaxation brings on sleep. He also said that only the breathing method eliminates muscle jerks that often accompany falling asleep. The jerk occurs at the moment you are passing into sleep. This causes you to be more wide awake than you were before starting to go to sleep.

Kelly was thorough so he did not neglect other aids to sleep. He urged careful attention to a bed that is firm and comfortable. A bed that is too soft makes turning more difficult and tends to heat the portion of the body that is sunk into it. A bed that is too hard causes the bones and joints to press against it uncomfortably. He was most concerned that the neck be in a proper position because the neck is so important during the day because it positions the head. Any strains in the numerous nerves of the neck are not only painful during the day, but interfere with sleep at night. A cramped neck can interfere with the blood supply to the brain and reduce the good that comes from sleep. The neck should be supported by a pillow or pillows that can keep the head and neck in the same position to the body at night that it is in during the day. This is especially needed for older persons whose joints and bones are more sensitive to position and pressure.

Kelly preferred going to sleep on one side or the other as a more relaxed position for the body and the spine. If there is a tendency toward bursitis, it is possible to put a pad under the body reaching almost to the shoulder in order to reduce the pressure on the shoulder joint. If the knees rest against each other to cause irritation, a pad should be put between them. Fatigue before going to bed helps bring sleep. Exercises and solitary walks in the evening help produce fatigue as well as quieting the excitement of the day.

Sleeping alone reduces the interruptions in beginning and continuing sleep. Relaxation before starting to sleep is suggested, including lifting and dropping the arms and legs on the bed. Sleep in a room that is as dark as and quiet as possible. If the room cannot be made quiet, noises can be muted with a continuous sound such as a fan or air conditioner. Eye blinders can be made from cloth and ear plugs can be made from cotton, rubber or soft wax.

Eye alertness is not only due to signals of light sent to the brain, but also comes from sending signals of eye muscle position to the brain. Long ago it was noticed, that individuals in deep sleep turned their eyes upward. The natural sleep position of the eyes is upward. Turning the eyes upward is a strong inducement to go to sleep. The eyes in that position also reduce the parade of images that cross the brain. Kelly recommended thinking black when lying down to sleep as an additional method of eliminating images. When you think everything is black, it is difficult to imagine any images. One further aid recommended is to take a daily rest period of five minutes sitting or lying quietly. If a catnap results, that is advantageous too.

Ventilation concerns some people in connection with sleep. Kelly said that ventilation is not a problem. Two people use only one—fourth of the oxygen in a sealed bedroom, 12' by 14', during a period of eight hours. No bedrooms are sealed from some ventilation around doors, windows, fixtures, cracks or porous plaster. In order to overcome your concern for getting enough air during controlled breathing, remember that your lungs are capable of furnishing far more osygen than you need. The lungs can hold a maximum of ten pints of air, but only one pint is breathed in and out during ordinary breathing. The lungs are capable of exhaling two pints of air above the normal one pint and can inhale five pints above the normal one pint. Two pints of air cannot be exhaled at all. Stuffy air is usually humid air rather than stale or exhausted air.

Variation one

Variation one in the Kelly method requires you to breathe in as much as possible, filling the diaphragm and expanding the chest completely. Then exhale as much as possible. Relax in the natural position a few seconds, then repeat the inhaling and exhaling in the same manner two more times. Then hold the breath until no longer comfortable. Upon inhaling again, repeat the three breath cycle again. The objective is to stop exhaling carbon dioxide and to allow it to build up in the blood and brain. There is no need to be concerned about the lack of oxygen, because the blood contains four or five times as much as the body needs to use during the period of holding the breath. After doing the three breath cycle for three more times, wait a few minutes before starting the next three breaths. The purpose of the breath holding after each three breaths is assisted by holding or moving the eyes upward with each breath as if you are looking at the rising of fireworks. Kelly also liked to repeat nursery rhymes while going to sleep.

Variation two

Variation two consists of inhaling as much as possible and exhaling as much as possible for three breaths, with a slight hesitation between breaths exactly the same as in variation one. Instead of holding the breath, breathe tiny breaths about one—third of your ordinary one pint of inhalation. Continue the tiny breaths until uncomfortable. Then repeat the three maximum breaths for another cycle. The purpose again is to retain carbon dioxide in the blood, but to avoid the tension caused by holding the breath in variation one. The method of three cycle breaths is cumulative. Continuing the process brings sleep closer. Each series of three breaths produces relaxation of the muscles and quiets the nervous system. Both of these two variations should be continued until they become natural. The first variation has the advantage of taking more concentration and effort. It may take your mind off the concerns you go to bed with. The second variation is more relaxing. Either variation may be continued until it brings sleep without harm. Both methods may be used together. When sleep is near, there is often an itching sensation around the nose and mouth which may be a signal to you that you are about to fall asleep. Nursery rhymes, childhood thoughts of being tucked into bed, pointing the eyes upward and thinking black may all help.

Variation three

Variation three starts the same as the other two by inhaling and exhaling as much as possible. Instead of holding the breath or taking tiny breaths, take the normal one pint breaths at one—half the usual rate. In order to do this, it is easiest to hold the finger on the pulse. Inhale to the count of four and exhale to the count of four. This will give about eight or nine breaths per minute. This causes a small decrease in the amount of oxygen in the blood but a considerable increase in the amount of carbon dioxide. Care has to be exercised to avoid taking deeper than usual breaths. This variation may be tried if the first two variations did not produce sleep. Kelly said that you may alternate variation one for three to five minutes. If you are still awake, try variation two from three to five minutes. Then try variation three for three to five minutes. If you have been so overwrought at the beginning that this alternation has not yet succeeded, there is nothing to stand in the way of repeating the whole process again. These variations will be more sucessful with continued use.

Variation four

Variation four works in cases of persistent sleeplessness. Instead of the three maximum breaths, you take twelve or more successive maximum breaths before taking the tiny breaths as in variation two, or breathing at the one—half normal rate as in variation three. The theory behind this method is more complicated.

The brain is very sensitive to keeping the correct level of carbon dioxide in the blood and notices the sharp decrease in the carbon dioxide level due to the many deep breaths of over-breathing. The brain seeks to protect itself from further loss of its supply of carbon dioxide by decreasing the speed of blood circulation in it, in order to prevent the escape of the remaining supply of carbon dioxide. It does this by causing its own blood vessels to contract, which slows the flow of blood to it. This also causes a reduction in the amount of oxygen that can reach the brain. Instead of a usual surplus of oxygen, suddenly there is a shortage of oxygen reaching the brain. At this sign the brain seeks to protect itself a second time by reducing the level of its own operation and consumption of oxygen. This time, as the brain's activity starts to slow down from shortage of oxygen, your breathing shifts from maximum breaths to minimum breaths. The brain starts to receive blood high in carbon dioxide. The high level of carbon dioxide, as usual, signals the brain to slow down. This is a second signal to slow down. If you are lucky enough to have the two signals for the brain to slow down at the same time or in quick succession, the brain should be thrown into a status of sleep almost instantaneously.

Kelly noted that not everyone finds success with this method. It is possible with some persons that the large number of deep breaths will produce excitement instead of relaxation. This method is also the one method of the four Kelly methods in which a muscular jerk or start may occur at the point of falling asleep.

One of the differences in theory between Kelly and other authorities was his insistence that complete relaxation is not necessary to bring sleep. He declared that it is sleep that brings relaxation instead of the other way around. He says that those with nervous tension or fatigue may wake up as tense and fatigued than they did when they went to bed. An example of relaxation following sleep, is the person who nods as he falls asleep in the sitting position. The nod and relaxation of the neck muscles follow sleep instead of coming before it.

Another point of difference is that Kelly claimed that relaxing the eyes by voluntary conscious effort was unsuccessful, if not impossible. He stated that tension in the eyes is caused by thoughts coming from the brain. Only if the parade of thoughts coming out of the brain can be stopped, will the eye tension be stopped. His method of stopping the parade of thought images going to the eyes was to cause the brain to get an increased supply of carbon dioxide by the decreased number of breaths.

Kelly's methods of getting to sleep are perhaps the easiest and the most rapid in reaching results if they work for you. Even in Kelly's methods, success is not automatic. Persistent application produces the best results. In his devotion to the phenomenon of natural carbon dioxide in the brain, Kelly noted that one of the best methods of stopping the brain's signal to continue the hiccup was to raise the level of carbon dioxide.

Chapter VII

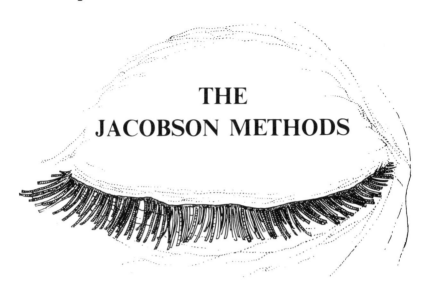

THE
JACOBSON METHODS

Dr. Edmund Jacobson instructed physicians how to teach patients to relax their muscles. He began experimenting in 1908, put out his first book in 1929 and his last revision about 1957. He addressed the problem of relaxation to obtain sleep as a treatment to be performed in a doctor's office. He did not have a high opinion of the advice or efforts of non-physicians. His system took sixty–eight hours of office training and could have been afforded only by the wealthy.

He begins by having the patient place his arm palm down on the table. The patient then bends his hand back to the limit and holds several minutes. Soon the feeling of tension is felt in the back of the arm. The patient should always remember this example of the sensation of tension. He should be able to recognize the same tension when it is present in any other muscle. Jacobson compares muscle tension to firing up an engine. Firing up the muscles produces the ashes of waste and extra pumping of blood to carry it away. Every added degree of tension puts a load on the heart and increases the blood pressure.

He asks the patient to form the habit of noticing his own muscle movements beginning with the first moment of awakening. All day long each muscle you contract causes the contraction of other muscles not needed for activity being done. This causes added tension to all other muscles.

The patient must learn to avoid all muscle movements that are unnecessary to the particular task he does. One result of such economy of effort is the reduction in the total number of muscles that are tensed in any one movement. All other muscles will also be less tense. If the patient watches the muscles involved in every movement to see which do tense, he will soon recognize the state of muscle tension and make note of it. Each day he will consciously reduce the number of muscles tensed and the degree of tension in the tensed muscles. Jacobson urged awareness of muscle use during work, play, reading, driving, telephoning and social activity. From this observation, the patient learns that muscle tension is his own doing. If a patient reaches the point of easily recognizing muscle tension and anxiety at any moment of the day, he will have learned enough to be able to turn it off.

Although Jacobson described relaxation as a field for doctors and doctors alone, he was willing for preparatory instruction to be given by trained school teachers. His description of the tensions in nearly every occupation gives the impression that almost everyone needs to become a Jacobson patient. He once gave instructions to five Navy commanders who were not physicians, in order that they might teach relaxation to others. They proceeded to teach other instructors how to teach the Jacobson method.

Jacobson defines fear as every effort made to meet situations successfully. This means that nearly every activity or intention we have may arouse a sense of fear. Fear of this kind may produce tension and anxiety. All mammals seek to remove irritation by leaving or changing their environment: by treating their ailments, by special foods or vitamins, by a new philosophy of life, by changing the amount of light or noise, by giving up smoking or alcohol, or by engaging in a hobby or sport. None of these efforts solves the problem of tension.

Overactive nerves are actually over tense muscles. The nervousness is due to the existence of too many tense muscles too much of the time. All the muscles are given two sets of nerves, one to carry messages to the muscle; the other to carry messages from the muscle to the brain. The speed is between forty and one hundred yards per second. The patient feeling overactive nerves imagines tumors, gland problems and a long list of other ailments.

Jacobson notes that when the tense patient goes to see some physicians, he is examined and told there is nothing wrong with him. But the patient can't forget his ailment. Such a person goes from physician to physician, getting treatment for one thing after another. He may even have an operation for his imaginary disease which is due solely to tense muscles.

Relaxation is the absence of all contraction. The muscle is so limp that it offers no resistance to stretching. Relaxation results in no muscle movement at all. There is lower pulse and breathing. The internal organs and blood vessel muscles relax. When the muscles are completely relaxed, the nerves carry no messages to or from the muscle. If you are tense a sudden noise causes a start, but if you are relaxed it will produce little or no start. Nervousness means busy nerves carrying messages. It is impossible to be nervous if the muscles are relaxed.

If a nervous person lies in bed, he may receive no restful results. You can lie in bed for hours, full of mental activity, excitement, emotion and anxiety demonstrated by fidgeting fingers and feet. Eyes and vocal equipment are active. Such rest is not complete. It does not refresh. Fatigue may not remove tension, but it does allow some sleep.

Jacobson used his method of relaxation to treat worry, depression and fear. Recovery came because relaxation results in less interest in the subject of the worry.

Jacobson said that self-suggestion or suggestion made by others is related to hypnosis. He urged the patient to avoid silent or vocal suggestion in learning to relax. He also urged against using yoga other derivatives of Asian meditation techniques. He was against autogenic self-suggestions. He did not say why he opposed any method except his own.

His treatments were for periods of one hour each for a total minimum of sixty—eight treatments, which will be described to be performed at home instead of in a doctor's office. The treatments are called progressive because they start with one set of muscles and progress on to other groups of muscles. The result of each treatment increases the level of relaxation.

Method one

The position is flat on the back, arms at the sides, but not touching the body; palms down, with or without a pillow; eyes closed, in a quiet room free from interruption. A small pillow may be placed under the knees.

The first exercise is to raise the left hand at the wrist bending it back toward the forearm for two minutes or more, without tensing any other muscles. Then let the hand drop entirely relaxed. Make no other movement. The purpose is to remember carefully what the tension felt like so you can recognize the same feeling when it occurs in other muscles. Repeat the same exercise again after two minutes. Wait and repeat it again. Spend the balance of the relaxation period lying quietly and try to recognize the sensation of tension in any of your muscles.

On the second day of exercise, after five or ten minutes of lying quietly, repeat the first exercise exactly as done before, paying attention to the feeling of tension in the back of the forearm. After a few minutes, press the left hand downward against the bed. If the bed is not resistant, place a book under your hand. Press downward for several minutes until the sensation of tension in the bottom of your forearm is obvious, then release. Repeat the exercise two more times. Spend the balance of your session lying quietly removing all the tension you can.

In the third session no exercise is performed. The whole period is spent lying quietly trying to make the left arm as relaxed as possible.

In the fourth session, rest for a few minutes as in the earlier sessions, then repeat the exercises of the first and second days. After a few minutes raise your left arm from the elbow. Hold it at an angle for two minutes until you clearly feel the tension in your upper arm. It will not be as plainly felt as it was when you raised the hand in the first exercise. Let the arm drop. Rest for a few minutes before repeating two more times. Rest the remainder of the period.

For the fifth session, repeat the exercises done in session four. In future sessions do not practice more than three previously performed exercises before starting the new exercise. Place a book under the left hand and press downward on it with the arm straight until the tension in the under part of the upper arm is felt, then release. Repeat the exercise two more times and remain quiet the remainder of the period.

In the sixth session, like the third, remain quiet the whole period and try to eliminate all tension.

The seventh session is a repetition of session one except that it is done with the right arm. The eighth session through the twelfth session repeat exercises two through six using the right arm. If you believe that you are succeeding in attaining complete relaxation as the exercises reach this point, you will be wrong. Various degrees of tension will still remain. During the exercises of the right arm, you may start using lesser degrees of tension as an experiment in recognizing less and less tension to the point where you scarcely move the hand or arm. Little by little this will teach you to recognize tension in a muscle down to a tiny amount. Later these tiny movements will be all that you will need to review the feeling of tension in a muscle.

The feeling of a relaxed muscle or group of muscles is difficult to notice. When the arm is completely relaxed, there won't be any feeling in the arm. Without looking, you may not be able to tell where the arm is. Some people are more sensitive to the feeling of tension than others and recognize it more easily.

Session thirteen begins the exercises of the right leg by bending the toes upward toward the knee, tensing the area on the front of the lower leg. Follow the same procedure as you did with the arms. Continue to use only the muscles required for the exercise without tensing any other muscles. In session fourteen, press the toes downward to tense the calf. Session fifteen is the quiet session.

In session sixteen the knee is placed on the edge of the bed with the lower leg held outward at an angle. All parts of the leg should be limp except the top of the thigh. In session seventeen, pull the heel of the bent leg toward the buttock in order to tense the back of the thigh. Session eighteen is the quiet session.

In session nineteen raise the straight leg upward from the bed to cause tension in the abdomen. You may prefer to raise the thigh only and let the lower leg hang limp from the knee and the heel resting on the bed. In the twentieth session press downward with the whole leg to tense the buttock area. The twenty−first session is the quiet session.

There are two sessions for the trunk; the first is to pull in the stomach, and the second to arch the back to feel the muscles. The twenty−fourth session is lying quietly, or trying minimal tensing of muscles to so slight a degree that the tensing is not visible.

The next session for the chest muscles is intended to teach recognition of the tightness of the chest by inhaling fully, feeling the muscles of the chest and then letting the chest fall naturally. Jacobson opposed the use of yoga and any other unnatural breathing methods on the grounds that they were not good for health.

One session is devoted to the shoulder in order to recognize three sets of muscles in three motions of the shoulder. First press the hands against the opposite shoulder and tense the front of the chest. Then pull the shoulders backward to tense the area of the shoulder blades. Next pull the shoulders upward.

The neck session is in four movements: front, back, right side and left side. The muscles should go limp after each exertion. Hunching the shoulders and straining the neck is often done all day, exhausting the muscles and tensing the whole speech area. Headaches and neck cricks may occur.

The face, the eyes and the speech equipment are the last groups of muscles in Jacobson's relaxation system. They are the most important of all the muscles in getting to sleep.

The first session is for the forehead muscles. Raise the forehead in order to notice the tension created, especially if the muscles are tensed in the raised position all day. The second session is for the frown muscles. The third group of muscles are the eyelids which are exercised by closing them hard in the Jacobson manner of three separate tensions. The forehead, frown and eyelid muscles are important in their relationship to the eye muscles and contribute to eye tension. If you can get relaxation in those three sets of muscles, eye tension control will be easier to reach.

The next session is for the eye muscles. Turn the eye right until tension is felt, then left, then up and then down. Repeat the exercise until the feeling is clear, each time trying to let the eyes go limp. So important is the eye in getting to sleep, Jacobson directed the eye exercise to be done for seven successive sessions. He urged becoming aware of eye tension during the day, in order to seek relaxation by changing eye activity. The eye muscles create tension in other muscles. One of the ways to induce relaxation in the eye is to tense the whole arm; relax it slowly and try to let the eye muscles go limp.

The second set of sessions on eye relaxation are also seven in number. Pretend you are watching a bird or an airplane fly. Look from one side as far as you can to the other side as far as you can look. All the sessions are devoted to becoming conscious of the existence of tension in the eye muscles and learning to decrease or eliminate it. When you can completely relax your eyes, mental images should stop.

The sessions dealing with the muscles of speech begin with tensing the cheek muscles. Pull the cheeks back to bare the teeth. The perpetual smile uses some of these muscles and tends to cause tension. The second set of muscles are the lips. Purse them by forming the letter "o". The third set are the jaw muscles. Clench the jaw and release. The jaw muscles are often clenched all day by grinding the teeth. This makes the jaw muscles difficult to relax at night, as well as causing tension during the day.

Two sessions are used for the tongue which is tensed by pulling it back and pressing it against the teeth. Three sessions are used for recognizing the feeling of tension in the throat muscles. Count to ten aloud in the first session, then reduce the volume more and more in the next two sessions almost to the point of counting mentally. In the last session you may try mental counting to see if you can feel any movement of the throat muscles. The throat muscles are delicate and require skilled attention in order to recognize the tension. Tension in the speech area leads to tension in the neck, chest and abdomen. Jacobson recommended five more sessions of practicing mental speech, consisting of imaginary conversations with those who are a part of daily your life. You should notice the appearance of tension without using audible sounds.

Jacobson said that only relaxation itself produces sleep and not much tension is present when sleep occurs. When the muscles of the eye and speech are relaxed, you are asleep. To assist in reaching this condition, it is advisable to do sitting exercises during the day, emphasizing the review of the eye and speech relaxation exercises. For the person who is a long time insomniac, it is important to reduce the daytime excitement of the muscles. The tension of the day carries over to bedtime and does not stop easily.

Method two

The starting position is the same as in method one. Lie on your back or on either side. Close the eyes in a darkened room free from noise, with your arms at your sides. Let the mind go blank. Folding the hands over the chest or abdomen is not advised because it increases the number of sensory messages going to the brain from the hands. The hands are richly supplied with nerve endings. The fewer the number of impulses the senses receive, the better it will be for doing the six types of exercises in this method. Use the size pillow you prefer.

Clench the right fist and raise the arm off the bed at a high angle, holding it with all muscles of the arm tense. Hold the arm in that position for one minute or until no longer comfortable. Let all the muscles relax suddenly so that the arm falls limp from its own weight. Wait a few minutes before tensing all the muscles of the arm while leaving it at your side. After a minute in this position, begin to let the muscles relax gradually. Repeat this exercise again, trying to reach as complete a state of relaxation as possible. As an alternative, raise both arms tensed and let them fall relaxed.

The second exercise consists of pushing the toes downward as far as they will go and holding them there a minute or until uncomfortable. Stop the tension suddenly. When letting go, try to reduce the tension in all the rest of the muscles of the body. If this exercise gives you a cramp in the calf, pull the toes as far upward toward the knees as you can. If you cramp easily from the exercise, you can use the pulling of the toes upward as an alternative. Repeat this exercise. The third time you do this exercise, let the toes relax slowly.

The third exercise deals with relaxation of the chest. Breathe in more deeply than usual, hold the breath and exhale slowly while relaxing the chest. Wait a moment and repeat several times. Most people do not realize they are tense in the chest until such an exercise teaches them to recognize chest tension. Jacobson believed that deep breathing does not put you to sleep. It simply increases the supply of oxygen to the brain.

Exercise four deals with the forehead. Raise the forehead for a moment, then letting it relax slowly. Squint the brow in a frown for a moment, then gradually relax the brow. Repeat this exercise and try to attain complete relaxation.

Exercise five is for the eyes. Turn the eyes as far to the right as possible for one–half a minute. Then let them relax free in their sockets without focusing on anything. Do the same exercise with the eyes looking to the left, looking up towards the forehead and looking downward, each time seeking to relax all muscles as you relax the eyes.

Exercise six is for muscles of the speech area. Count aloud to ten, being aware of the muscles of the throat, tongue and jaw. At the count of ten let them all go limp. Repeat the exercise using a lower and lower volume of counting. Finally count to ten mentally, trying not to use the muscles of the throat.

Jacobson said that some people could learn to relax enough under this system to control sleep in a few weeks. Some people might take months, but after a year of practice, your sleep would come easily for the rest of your life. After successfully mastering this method, doing all of the above exercises would no longer be necessary. Doing one of the steps should trigger all the steps of relaxation at once, making your body ready for sleep. Uninterrupted practice should be maintained because stopping will cause you to lose some skill.

Jacobson claimed other uses of his method besides help in getting to sleep. One other use was the reduction of blood pressure. He suggested that as many as one hundred visits to his office might be necessary to learn to keep the blood pressure down permanently. Another use was the reduction in ailments of the digestive system caused by too much tension, including the most common of all digestive complaints; tightness or a lump in the lower throat. He recommended lying down for a few minutes before each meal. Strain throughout the day not only reduces the amount that can be accomplished during the day, but interferes with the process of getting to sleep.

An example was given of a corporation executive who was advised to relax. Each time he returned from repeated short vacations, he was refreshed for only the first day. After that he was as exhausted and sleepless as before the vacations. After three months of the Jacobson steps, his symptoms of tension and sleeplessness had disappeared without any vacation.

Chapter VIII

DR. FINK'S METHOD

David H. Fink was first a college teacher, then an athletic coach, then a social worker and finally went to medical school. His approach to sleep was a combination of relaxation and self-suggestion at the same time. He emphasized the importance of relaxation to your health and to your effective work output. He said that tension prevents you from thinking clearly, seeing sharply and hearing acutely.

He recommends lying flat on your back, using four pillows: one under your neck, one under your knees and one under each elbow. The head and neck must be comfortable or all efforts to relax into sleep will fail. The head should tip back a small amount with the neck supported. The knee pillow takes tension away from the muscles of the back of the thigh and relieves the tension in the knee joint. The legs are not to be straight, but tipped slightly toward the outside so that they almost rest on the outside of the calves. Place the elbows eight or nine inches away from the body and the hands next to the body. In your ordinary sleeping room, close your eyes, let your jaw sag, and allow your lips to barely touch.

Dr. Fink's sleep technique is divided into ten individual steps.

One week of practice is devoted to each step. Step one is addressed to the arms. Each time you breathe out, say to your arms, "Let go," and "Let go more." You do not need to say it out loud. Say it mentally and distinctly to yourself. Follow the same procedure each night. Fink noted that there is a connection between successful performance of any physical activity and verbalization of the performance. This process starts in childhood when children are taught to perform activities by verbal directions. Later they learn by talking to themselves and still later, they teach themselves by reading directions. Muscular action is frequently a conditioned reflex to words you say to yourself or that you hear.

After doing step one for a week during the period before going to sleep, start step two in the same way by relaxing your arms for three or four minutes. Then begin giving verbal directions to your chest with every exhalation saying, "Let go," and "Let go more." Pay no attention to the way you inhale and exhale, except to do it naturally. You may insist that you know how to relax, but by the end of the second week you will have discovered tense muscles you never knew you had. You will realize that you have never really relaxed before. Some individuals feel a slight tingling in the area that they have learned to relax. This is caused by the increased circulation of blood permitted by the newly relaxed blood vessels. After relaxation has been learned, you will usually notice that your hands are warmer than before.

After practicing the chest relaxation procedure for one week, start the third step by three or four minutes of the arm relaxation and the chest relaxation. Then address yourself to your shoulders each night for a week. Say mentally but clearly to your shoulders, "Let go," and "Let go more," each time you exhale. Each night practice the previous steps before starting the shoulders procedure. By the end of the third week you should be going to sleep with no difficulty at all. Often this is the time when individuals stop taking further steps. But if you want success in getting to sleep as well as being able to relax all day long, continue the program to the end.

Begin step four with the usual short practice of the previous steps in relaxing arms, chest and shoulders. Next say to the muscles of your back, from the small of your back on upward, "Let go," and "Let go more." Do this for one week.

Step five begins with a short practice of the previous steps. Then address yourself to the muscles of the legs. Concentrate as usual on saying to your legs, "Let go," and "Let go more."

One of the things you will have noticed as you have continued your procedure is that your breathing rate has decreased. It may decrease as much as one-half in deep relaxation. This occurs without any conscious effort on your part. It is evident that the lower level of tension in the different parts of your body is decreasing the expenditure of energy by your muscles. There is a decrease in the force your heart has to exert in order to drive the blood through your tiny blood vessels. Your metabolism has decreased. In a sense your body has started to discontinue fighting its muscles against each other.

Step six is directed at the muscles of the neck. Start with your usual routine of reviewing each of the previous exercises briefly. You may have noticed that upon rehearsing each of the previous weekly steps, just turning your thought to a group of muscles will trigger relaxation in them. No longer do you have to spend much time trying to get your arms to relax. The farther you progress, the quicker your self-suggestion will enable you to find complete relaxation and sleep as you perform the exercises. Ultimately you will have the ability to trigger the whole ten weeks of relaxation practice into a single thought pattern.

The seventh step is directed to relaxing the face muscles. After your review of the previous steps, direct the words, "let go," and "let go more," toward each group of muscles that you can identify in your face. In any of these exercises, do not try hard to relax. Trying hard causes tension. One of the frequent causes of sleeplessness is the anxiety or anger aroused in a person who says to himself, "Now I am going to force myself to go to sleep." You are attempting to reverse the habit patterns and mental procedures of your life in a short period of time. The only way to imprint the new attitudes and habits is by repetition without letting the old habits renew themselves. In the present step you are trying to relax the muscles of your face. With persistence you will notice the lines of your face becoming less tight. A greater appearance of repose will affect your daily life.

The eighth step is devoted to your scalp and forehead. Review your previous exercises before addressing your mental language to let go toward your scalp. Scalp tension is most evident in animals which can make their fur stand up, but we have muscles that are comparable.

The ninth week deals with the two most difficult sets of muscles to control. They are the muscles of the eyes and the speech area. Review the previous exercises very briefly. Then say to your eye muscles, which number six in each eye, "Let go," and "Let go more." Try to make them so loose that they feel like they are going to fall out of their sockets.

One of the reasons the eye and speech muscles are left to the last is so that you will have developed enough skill to undertake the difficult problem of relaxing them. You have probably begun to notice that not only are you more skilled at getting to sleep, but you are finding your sleep more restful. You feel better upon awakening and during the day. You may even find that you need to sleep less than you did before.

For the tenth week, after your review of the other steps, mentally address your speech muscles as softly as you can with the words, "Let go," and "Let go more." You may also tell them to be calm. As you continue the speech muscle exercise during the week, remember that ten weeks is a very short time to accomplish a retraining of your attitudes and muscular habits. Any interruption of practice will allow the old habits to reassert themselves. Continue to do your exercises after the end of the ten weeks, spending more time on the muscles that seem to insist on returning to tension. Now you can recognize a tense muscle which you formerly could not do.

If you can give yourself directions to sleep, as you have been doing, you can give yourself other directions before you go to sleep. You can say to yourself several times, usually once with each exhalation, "I am going to sleep relaxed the whole night." It will work for you. Your brain is waiting for you to give it directions. Your brain may carry out these directions after you have forgotten that you gave them. Giving yourself directions before going to sleep is called controlled sleep.

The directions you give to yourself can be for matters other than going to sleep. You decide what you want to do, within limits of reasonable possibility. As you doze off, you can be repeating to yourself over and over, "Tomorrow cigarettes will nauseate me." It will not be long before your brain has taken care of your smoking problem without great daytime efforts by you. You can try the same technique for eliminating other habits or characteristics. Keep the verbalizations positive in tone rather than negative. Apply the same principles you have used in the first ten steps.

It is possible for you to speed up the process of relaxing into sleep during the ten weeks of basic practice by doing daytime exercises. During the daytime you can do the extra exercises while you are in a sitting position. Your chair should be low. Sit as far back in a straight chair as possible, feet flat on the floor, body upright, arms dangling at your sides, eyes half open or closed. The verbal directions are the same as when you are doing the exercises in bed. Say to your arms, "Let go," and "Let go more." Say the same thing to your shoulders. Go on to your chest, legs, neck, eyes and speech area. Two minutes or five minutes of this will make a difference. Do this twice a day if possible. You can try this exercise as you sit in your car. You can even do some good while you are waiting at a stop light, keeping your eyes open. Hold the steering wheel lightly, applying the minimum muscular tension required to accomplish the activity you are doing. These exercises can be continued on a permanent basis.

Muscular tension is, in large part, an expression of emotion. It becomes habitual in response to daily activity. The emotional state ends when the relaxation occurs. The development of relaxation should be accomplished by weak signals from you. A strong signal may cause the opposite reaction. The signal, "Let go" is a weak signal. When you tell yourself that you have to do something right now, the reaction is resistance.

When you try to turn your long time habitual behavior patterns which have been producing your daily tensions, you must expect to turn them only a degree at a time. Each degree will make the next degree easier. Eventually the cumulative result of your efforts will be success in overcoming the tensions and emotions that have inhibited your daily activity and you will achieve restful sleep.

Dr. Fink, with his modern approach, has produced a synthesis of several of the other established methods of going to sleep. Because his method embraces the essentials of the meditative method, the autogenic method, the progressive relaxation method and the self-hypnosis method, it may attract more and more adherents.

Chapter IX

MEDITATION
INTO
SLEEP

The practice of meditation is found in every society, culture and religion. The ancient Egyptians, Greeks, Romans and Hebrews were aware of it. The early Christians formalized forms of it. From them the Moslem forms of meditation arose. The colonization of southern Asia led to a wider awareness of meditation. Meditation appears to be part of the common human experience.

The purposes of meditation include seeking relaxation, sleep, well being, selflessness, peace of mind, self-examination, ability to concentrate, greater will power, self-discipline, and greater efficiency in daily life. There are also mystical purposes such as religious contemplation, adoration of God, clairvoyance, ecstasy and the extravagant muscle controls found in India. The Quakers have Inner Light, the Sufis have Fana, Zen has Satori and the Yogis have Samdhi.

The natural result of the meditation process is sleep. Long time practitioners of a commercially taught form of meditation indicated in response to a questionnaire, that daytime meditation from a sitting position in twenty minute periods, results in sleep more than forty percent of the time. Because their objective is to avoid going to sleep, the percentage who go to sleep without wanting to may be even higher, as some may not realize they are sleeping. The difficulty of staying awake in the upright posture of meditation has been recognized in the literature of all the Christian, Jewish, Sufi, Yoga, and Zen methods. To avoid going to sleep while lying in bed and meditating is almost impossible.

All peoples have recognized that tension is damaging to the health of the body functions and to physical and mental performance.

The antidote for tension is relaxation. The major product of meditation is relaxation. Meditation is aimed at mentally applying influence to the body and mind in order to decrease the activity of the autonomic nervous system. The autonomic nervous system controls the speed of organ operation and the metabolic rate. All of the meditation methods slow the metabolic furnace, the electric impulses in the brain and nerves, the pulse, the blood pressure, the muscular tension and the glandular secretions.

Meditation can be learned entirely from the written word. A teacher can be helpful, but no teacher is better than a poor teacher. A poor teacher is a non-professional person who does not have any interest in you as a person, doesn't know your daily concerns and cannot evaluate how you are doing. If someone tells you that his method of meditation is the only one that works, stay away.

In any form of meditation, do not expect the same experience that anyone else has. Meditation will give you no major changes in your personality, but it will make you less anxious, less suspicious and less hostile. You may have to try several methods before you find the one that fits you best. As with exercise, practice will produce results. Try each method for two or three weeks to find out if it feels right for you. If you do not like it, try another. Read the instructions several times before starting a method; then read them over once a day for a week. The fact that a method works well one night does not mean that it will work well every night.

The general classification of meditation methods are those that use breath counting, those that use a word or phrase as a focus of attention, those that use an idea as a focus of attention, those that use a body function as a focus of attention and those that solely seek emptiness of mind and absence of thought.

All forms of meditation for sleep start from the position that you have found to be the most successful in inducing sleep. If you have no usual position, lie on your back in a comfortable position, with such pillows as are needed to keep the head and neck supported in a non-strained attitude toward the body. The knees should be bent enough to avoid putting tension on the back of the legs and on the back bone. Turn the eyes upward and hold them without causing tension during the meditation.

The counting method

Method one concentrates on the counting of breaths, making a count of one for each exhalation. The breathing does not have to be done in a manner different from normal, but will probably settle down to longer and deeper breaths than usual. Let go all your muscles as if letting your whole body collapse as you exhale each breath. Direct all of your attention to the counting and turn your mind away from any other thoughts. You will find that this is impossible to do completely because the mind flits continually from one subject to another. Bring your mind gently back to concentration on the counting. The counting may be done aloud or mentally. Some practitioners recommend counting only up to four and then starting over. This makes the activity more repetitive and requires less concentration on what the next number should be. You may make the small variation of using the word "and" with each inhalation between numbers. You may count up to ten and then start over again. Do not be concerned about how difficult it is to keep your mind on counting. Because the thoughts will wander, it is better to think of the contentment of sleeping all night. This is the simplest method with which to start your meditation experience. You may not need another method. If you do, wait until you have done method one for two or three weeks before trying another. The gradual effects of learning to control your thoughts and being able to concentrate will overflow, improving all the activities of your life.

Simple as the breath counting method is, it teaches how to accomplish one thing at a time. As you get more control over your thoughts, you will get more control over your life. You will feel lighter, less cramped and full of natural vitality. When you feel less tight, your senses will be more receptive and keen. As you are able to think about subjects important to you long enough to understand them, you will learn how to accomplish your goals.

Mantra meditation

Method two starts from the same comfortable position in bed as before, free as possible from disturbances. This is the meditation of concentration on a single word. The commercial transcendental method is an offshoot of this. In this method counting breaths can be ignored. Your breathing will gradually become slower and deeper. Relaxation will spread to all areas of the body, increasing a little with each exhalation. The mind will wander off the mantra word every few seconds, but you are not to be concerned about that. The better attitude is to be amused. Each time bring the mind back to concentration on saying the word.
Choose a word on which to concentrate. It is more effective if the word is meaningless. Throughout history words and phrases with religious meanings have been the most frequently used, but not for the purpose of attracting sleep. The word should be relaxing to say, using as few muscles of speech as possible. Either aloud or mentally shape the mouth and throat for the word. The traditional word of India has been "om", but the word requiring the least muscular effort is "ah" or "hah." Such a sound requires almost no tensing of any muscles. Other examples are "Awe," "Haw," "Hawm," "Hawn," "Hahm," "Hahn," "Hoo," "Hoon," "Hoom," "How," "Howm" and "Hown." One of the more successful words for sleep meditation is "drowse." Continue to use your word or mantra for a week or more, expressing it with each exhalation. If you like it, make it a trigger word which will put your mind and body into the meditation state almost instantaneously.
The requirements for this method may be summarized as an absence of external distractions, a comfortable, motionless position in bed, a word for the mind to concentrate on and a passive attitude. In India where the dust was thick during the dry season, all meditation methods called for breathing through the

nose, but the literature of meditation techniques in the western world, do not have directions about nose breathing. Relaxation is more complete with the jaw loose and the throat open.

Floating log method

In Method three, start with the same position. You are to imagine that your bed is overlooking a stream. You are mentally watching the water go by containing an occasional log floating slowly downstream. The object of the floating log technique is to assign each separate thought to a log and to hold the attention on that thought for the four to ten seconds it takes for the log to float out of sight. The proper sequence is to mentally put a log in the stream with the arrival of each new thought. Then concentrate on the thought as the log goes by. Do not think of the log as such, but as your thought which you will keep in mind to the exclusion of all other thoughts during the time the log is passing by. It is all right if the same thought repeats. Any thought or concept that comes is suitable. If thoughts tend to be about sleep, pleasant childhood mental pictures of going to bed or how drowsy you are, so much the better, but no controls should be placed on the thoughts that may come.

The dvantage of the floating log technique is that it sets a definite period of time for the duration of the thought. You tend to hold your attention for a known quota of time so that it is easier to avoid the interruption of other thoughts. There is no need for the stream of thoughts to contain ideas that are related to each other.

A variation of Method three is to picture yourself lying in your bed before a glass window that looks into a tank or pond such as are used for underwater displays. Bubbles will rise slowly through water. When a thought arrives, let a bubble start from the bottom of the tank or pool to the surface for four to ten seconds. Hold your mind on the single thought while the bubble rises, turning away other intruding ideas. As with other meditation techniques, the aim is for the mind to do or think one thought at a time. A third variation is to think of your bed being situated before a campfire into which you are looking. For each puff of smoke that rises out of the fire and dissipates, assign a thought that comes to mind. As each new thought arrives, start a new puff of smoke and hold off other thoughts for the few seconds it takes for the puff to dissipate. Whatever method you find most comfortable for you, settle down to that method so that it becomes a part of you. As with any activity, skill develops slowly. Eventually you will look back and marvel at how awkward you were at the beginning.

Hub of the wheel meditation

Method four is called the central theme or the hub of the wheel technique. You start by choosing a central concept for the hub such as slumber, sleep, doze, comfort, sweet repose, bed or any other concept you wish to use in connection with contented sleep. With your mind on that central concept, notice the first new thought that comes along. Hold that new thought long enought to see if there is any connection between it and the central theme. Then return to the central thought until the next new thought arrives. Compare it with the central hub idea for any association. There may be or may not be any connection. It makes no difference. Return again to the central hub thought.

As you can see, this method differs from the last method of the floating log. In this method there is a connection between the thoughts since each of them tends to be influenced by the central hub thought. Sometimes the same thought will return a second time. Although no association with the hub was seen the first time, an association is seen the second time around. Endeavor to make all the central hub thoughts as pleasant and enjoyable as you can, because they tend to create a mood. This method may yield new insights to you about yourself.

If you sometime see strange visualizations similar to hallucinations or dreams when you meditate, pay no attention to them. The purpose of meditation is not to see irrelevant visions, but to sleep.

Body functions

The fifth method is quite different. Concentration is not on an idea or word, but on a movement or function of the body. You may feel the beat of the pulse or take notice of the movement of breathing, while shutting out your attention to anything else. Instead of thinking of an idea or a word, this method of meditation is non-visual and non-verbal. You feel the function such as the pulse with the finger, imagining that it is the sleeping pulse. You also feel the breath with the hand or hands on the diaphragm. In each case the aim is to concentrate on the feeling of the function. Bring the mind back to the feeling every time it moves into any idea or thought. Though you can exercise control of the rate and amount that you breathe, it is recommended that you do not exercise any effort to control the heartbeat.

Body concentration

Meditation in Method four starts from the same position as all the other methods. Lie on the back with a pillow under the neck, head and knees. A roll of blanket or other material may be used under the knees instead of a pillow. In this method, be aware of feeling that you are sinking deeper into the bed with every exhalation. At the same time try to feel limp. In this method your mind will concentrate for a short time on successive parts of the body. Bring the mind back each time it wanders from concentration on the particular part of the body.

Start with the right foot, keeping your mind fixed on it as much as possible for about one minute. At the same time think of the foot sinking deeper into the bed and getting limp. Do the same with the left foot, the calves, the thighs, the buttocks, the stomach, the back, the hands, the arms, the shoulders, the neck, the face, the jaw, the eyes and the throat. If you are still not asleep, you may continue concentrating on your breathing, while sinking deeper into the bed and feeling more limp with each exhalation. This method should be very relaxing and comforting, giving a sense of inner quiet. It relaxes tense muscles of which we are ordinarily not aware. Assume that contented sleep is signalling to you during the whole period of the meditation.

In all these methods, as the weeks go by, you will discover shortcuts to the goal you seek. These will be trigger thoughts, words or feelings that enable you to attain sleep more quickly.

Chapter X

THE
ROON TECHNIQUE
FOR SLEEP

The Roon method of overcoming insomnia is a combination of philosophy, psychology, exercise and common sense. Besides concentrating on the period before bedtime, Roon's method is directed at all the waking hours. Karin Roon was born in 1890 and became famous in several European countries as a physical therapist. In 1939 she began anew in the United States. She was a person whose energetic influence seemed to cause the problems of her followers to melt away.

Karin Roon's manner of daily living will produce good sleep as effectively as her specific sleep technique. She gave a body of advice to poor sleepers that had specific bedtime technique, but her true intention was to provide a technique that lasted all day.

Karin Roon's advice for daytime living

Tension is everybody's problem. Take a minute here and there all day long. Yawn wide with your jaw on your chest, keeping your eyes closed. Shake your jaw from side to side. This will relax your jaw, your mouth and your tongue. It will take away your frown. Your mouth can reveal you as determined, compressed, tense, discontented or pleasant. Follow the yawn with several good deep breaths, inhaling on one, exhaling on two and holding on three. Try to be limp and passive. Tension produces shallow breathing. The loose jaw is needed for good speech and to prevent placing strain on the larynx. Many persons are not even aware of their tensions. Make it a habit to keep your tongue relaxed behind your lower teeth.

A fixed, tight smile produces a tight throat and a tight chest. Tense persons develop a tense voice. Better breathing produces better work. Deep breathing helps dissipate anxiety. Whistling in a quiet manner improves the breathing and exercises the diaphragm. Lie down sometime during the day, stretching everything you can. Breathe deeply. This is just as important to persons at home all day as to those who are away. Before meals take a few deep breaths and loosen up.

Get the body into proper alignment by standing with your back to the wall. Keep that general posture in sitting, working and walking. You will find that it reduces fatigue, tension and backache. Do not cross the arms in front of you because it rounds the back and pulls the shoulders and shoulder joints out of position, tensing the muscles. Shake your hands from time to time as if there were water on them. Do not cross your knees or legs because this causes tension and is poor for the joints of the knees and the hips. Tense the buttocks when sitting from time to time. It's good for stomach ulcers, the kidneys and the liver. It also strengthens the back, improves your posture and the appearance of the buttocks.

Close your eyes at work occasionally and pretend they are so loose they could drop out or fall inward. Eye strain wears you out. Blink the eyes to reduce their tension. Change their focus, looking at the distance now and then. Reach as far as you can and then stretch all the joints and muscles several times a day. Even wiggling your toes in your shoes may reduce your tension.

Being rushed is not a virtue of good management. Plan your day. The greater your ability to relax, the more you can accomplish. Follow your own rhythm and let it be your guide to your rate of work. Do not try too hard in your work. Going too fast breaks your rhythm and produces both tension and fatigue.

Avoid seeking the unattainable. Business success is said to depend eighty percent on your personality and only twenty percent on your ability. It is the relaxed person who gets the job and gets it done. Keep your supply of energy in a natural balance so that your body and brain will work at their best.

Whatever your fears may be, millions of other persons have the same ones. Fear of being over-weight increases your hunger. Fear of losing your attractiveness causes the tension that attacks your appearance. Fear of age adds to tension that ages you. Some of the greatest charmers of the world were ugly.

Wasted energy fatigues us unnecessarily as it reduces the quality and quantity of our performance. An example of the body being at a high tension level accompanied by the exertion of unneeded force is the death grip many persons apply to the steering wheel of an auto. A relaxed car driver is the safest car driver. If you commute on public transportation, close your eyes. Just avoiding talk helps relaxation. Much handwriting is poor because too much force is applied to the pen. It is never too late to learn to relax. Often it is the tense rigid person who breaks down under pressure instead of the gentle relaxed person.

Keep a positive attitude. Tight muscles tend to cause a negative attitude, and can create a sense of fear. High tension pulls you toward a feeling of inferiority and encourages worry. Tension interferes with concentration at work and the functions of the internal organs. Tension prevents a sense of humor. It increases suspicion, holding of grudges and blame. It hinders the expression of your good emotions. Relaxation gives you flexibility to meet your problems plus better health and peace of mind. It enables you to attain a state of happiness and harmony with your surroundings.

Keep your finances in order. There is no other cure for financial worry except bringing your expenses within your income. The ideal sense of financial security is to live on the income you made the previous year. Spend only what you earned last year and bank all of this year's income until next year. The satisfaction and freedom from tension that you get out of this kind of security is greater than anything you can get from living beyond your income. People can have peace of mind on a low income, while people with high incomes can be in a constant state of financial worry. Financial worry is a deterrent to good sleep, good work and good health.

Karen Roon's sleep technique

Everyone has trouble getting to sleep once in a while. To cure insomnia, you have to want to end it. The best preparation for sleep is a long walk or other exercise, preferably by yourself. The color of your bedroom has an influence on you. Red colors are stimulating and blue or green colors tend to be sedative. The Roon basic condition is to put aside all problems and concerns before lying down. Nighttime ideas are distorted and unreliable. If they do wander into bedtime they should be restricted solely to the future. Think also about childhood scenes of warmth, for instance being tucked into bed.

Start with stretching and yawning. The mind should be concentrated on emptiness, the jaw slack, the breathing deep and slow, the eyes turned upward, the tongue loose. Do not try hard to go to sleep. Take a "don't care" attitude. Do not read unless it is something dull and uninteresting, such as the multiplication table. The less you lood at newspapers, news magazines and TV in the evening the better. If you wake up, do not start thinking. Be strict with yourself. Do not move around in bed. Practice slow deep breathing. Feel contented and sleep will come over you.

Chapter XI

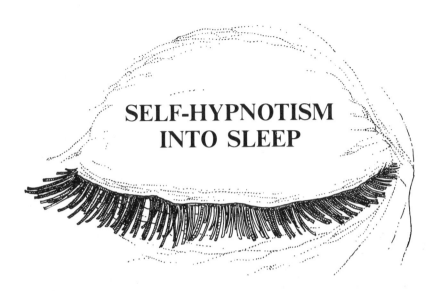

SELF-HYPNOTISM
INTO SLEEP

Self-hypnotism has been used from the earliest times of human existence. Individuals doing self-hypnosis believed they were either performing a natural function, making contact with a deity or summoning up ancestral spirits. Self-hypnosis happens during every daydream or reverie you have. Being totally absorbed in a hobby is a type of self-hypnosis as is concentration on TV or reading. When you lose your total concentration on your activity, the self-hypnosis dissipates without any other action on your part.

Modern awareness of hypnotism began with Dr. Franz Mesmer of Vienna, nearly a century before the word hypnotism was adopted. The treatment he gave to his patients was referred to as animal magnetism. Competitive Vienna doctors were so hostile to his talent and success that he felt compelled to leave the city. He went to Paris where his practice was just as successful, but his enemies obtained the appointment of a government body to decide if he could continue. Benjamin Franklin was a member of the commission which condemned Mesmer's treatment in 1784. Dr. Mesmer dropped out of sight and died discredited, but his method and concept survived him.

Health practitioners in the United States have had a tiny number of followers of Mesmer since 1823. By 1840 doctors and dentists in Boston were being shown its use in treatment. Dr. Esdaile from England described over 3,000 operations that took place under hypnosis in a hospital in India. Upon his return to England, his fellow doctors succeeded in taking away his license to practice. Dr. Elliotson, who invented the stethoscope, was likewise removed from practice because he used mesmerism. The development of anesthetics in 1846 ended the further spread of medical interest in hypnotism. Not until 1958 did the American Medical Association vote for recognition of hypnotism provided it was done by trained doctors.

If you are hypnotized, you know what is going on all the time. You are not unconscious. You can hear, talk and move around. You do not lose control of yourself. You will not do anything you are unwilling to do. No one but a criminal would be influenced to commit criminal acts while under hypnosis.

The more intelligent you are, the easier it is for you to become hypnotized. Morons cannot be hypnotized. There is no universal identifiable feeling that comes with hypnosis except lethargy. In a light stage, you may deny that you could have been in hypnosis. Hypnosis is not done by means of the eyes, as is proved by a professional hypnotist who is blind.

One authority, Dr. D.X. Barber, is quoted as having said that hypnosis does not require a trance. All you have to do is tell the subject to relax and give him suggestions of what to do. The person follows the suggestion if he is determined to do what the hypnotist suggests. For the subject, it is just a question of letting himself go.

Another authority, Dr. Andrew Salter, says hypnosis is the use of words to trigger a reflex action; that is, hypnosis is the result of a conditioned reaction to habit patterns you already have. He says that the hypnotized subject does not do anything except react to words such as, tired, sleep, warm, heavy, floating, drifting or comfortable. If you do not respond automatically to the meaning of the words used, then you cannot be changed by them under hypnosis. The word "suggestion" is the name for accomplishing the triggering of the conditioned reaction. Dr. Salter also agrees that the existence of a trance is not required for self-hypnosis.

Self-hypnosis is, in a sense, a state of concentration. When your whole conscious mental apparatus is concentrated on sleeping and you hold your focus on getting that result, self-hypnosis is the result. There can be no wandering of attention. You often engage in this process without being aware of it. For instance you may receive painful bruises and even sprains without knowing when or how, because you were totally concentrated on something else at the time of the injury. You were in deep enough self-hypnosis to be anesthetized. One theory is that all hypnosis is self-induced. The hypnotist only gives suggestions to you that you relay to your subconscious mind as your own suggestion. The conscious part of your mind does your thinking and directing. The subconscious part of your mind receives orders from you that can go through to the conscious part. The subconscious contains all your memories and can produce facts that have been forgotten by your conscious mind. We get the subconscious mind to perform this function when we ask it to find someone's name which we have forgotten. Sooner or later the subconscious mind suddenly produces the name we have asked for. The subconscious mind is a miracle of efficiency. It operates all the automatic functions we have, including walking, balancing, digestion; our heart, lungs, liver, kidneys, stomach and reflex actions. You can give your subconscious mind activities that it can perform more effectively than your conscious mind. If you had to direct all the muscles you need to cross the room, you probably would never get there.

Tension interferes with the operation of the subconscious mind. It is through tension that the subconscious mind causes most of the ailments and illnesses we have. Your subconscious mind can be protected by relieving yourself of tension. Tension blocks the pathway for your requests and directions to your subconscious mind. When the barrier protecting the subconscious mind is lowered by relaxation and patience, your self-hypnosis suggestions can reach it.

Anyone can learn self-hypnosis. Several methods of self-hypnosis will be described that you can use. The beginning position for all methods is to lie flat in bed, with or without a pillow, hands open, arms at your sides and in a quiet room. Breathe deeply for two minutes and fix your eyes on one point in the ceiling or on an imaginary point. Try to let go of all your muscles and concerns and close your eyes. Without forcing your mind, try to keep from being distracted. Concentrate for ten seconds on relaxing your right hand, your left hand, your right foot, your left foot, your face, lips, mouth and tongue. Keep yourself motionless. If you are not relaxed, repeat the concentration for ten seconds on each of the same points again a time or two. When you are relaxed, you are ready for self-hypnosis suggestions to start. Say mentally to yourself, "I am going to learn this technique. I am going to learn to fall asleep." Repeat several times. Next say to yourself several times, "I am very comfortable and I want to sleep." Then say, "I am beginning to fall asleep." The words of suggestion may be your own.

Self-hypnotizing suggestions should be framed in a tone of, "I can," "I am going to" or "I will soon." They should be permissive rather than mandatory. Suggestion works better than command. It also takes time for your suggestion to reach your computer-like subconscious mind, get the chemistry going to effect the change and go into effect. Not until you have had practice, will suggestions to your subconscious mind be quickly executed. A third reason for permissive phraseology is that beginners will be slower in getting results than habitual self-hypnotizers. The erroneous conclusion of the beginner is that he has not succeeded in getting into light self-hypnosis when he has. You should have absolute confidence that you will succeed. You should not attempt too much in the beginning. Suggestions should be framed for the minimum objective at first. If you fail in accomplishing bigger tasks than you have the ability to do, your confidence might decrease. You will begin to notice that you are getting results by the fourth night of practice, if not sooner. After many nights of practice in self-hypnosis, you should expect to be able to enter it within one minute. By that time the process will be so well imprinted on your mind as a habit pattern, you will be able to trigger yourself into self-hypnosis as a conditioned reaction to your mental suggestions.

A second technique for entering self-hypnosis is also elementary. You should begin as before, lying flat in a comfortable position, arms at your sides, breathing relaxed and more deeply than usual and gazing at a single imaginary spot. Close your eyes letting go all of your muscles and concerns, noticing the feeling of relaxation. Continue to mentally think, "let go" as you raise your right arm a few inches. Let it drop as you exhale. Raise your left arm a few inches and let it drop as you exhale. Arch your back a small amount, concentrating on letting go. Do not tense the muscles of your neck, mouth, face, lips and tongue, but think briefly of letting each of them go as you concentrate on each one separately. Finally let your eyes focus on an imaginary spot on your own forehead or hairline. When your eyes feel fatigued, let them go completely relaxed.

Each set of muscles that you relax should carry you a little deeper into self-hypnosis and prepare you for being able to give suggestions to your subconscious mind. Do not expect dramatic results on the first few nights. You may make the following suggestions to yourself: "I am going to find it easier to relax," "My patience will increase each day," "I will carry out my practice every night," "I will keep my thoughts on pleasant things" or "Things that formerly disturbed me will leave me unaffected." You can add the suggestion, "I am going to fall asleep soon." Repetition is just as important in this process as it is in advertising and selling.

One of the things that interferes with success in reaching self-hypnosis is to try too hard. It is also possible for you to use suggestions that are not acceptable to your particular subconscious mind, in which case you have to change the language. You should avoid using a negative form of suggestion such as, "This is not deep enough," or "I am not getting what I expected." Your subconscious mind operates on the positive directions given to it and is not fashioned to react to negative orders.

Avoid using the word "try" in your suggestions. The word "try" implies doubt in your mind. Belief hastens your success. It may help you to find a visual image while you are repeating your main suggestion, such as the image of yourself sound asleep in complete comfort. Your suggestions should avoid exact detail. When you let your subconscious know what you want, it will produce your result with suitable details to suit you. One problem may be to dehypnotize yourself from your negative attitudes and emotions in order for you to be able to receive positive suggestions. Stop a moment and examine yourself to see if this applies to you. After some experience you will find that you can shorten the whole process and reach light self-hypnosis simply by closing your eyes and counting slowly to ten.

A third method of reaching self-hypnosis is to lie in the same comfortable position used in the previous methods and think in a relaxed way that you are going to hypnotize yourself. Take five deep breaths mentally saying to yourself, "I will soon be fast asleep." Then concentrate on the following suggestions, repeating them for as long as five minutes: "I am very comfortable, so very comfortable. My arms are relaxed. My feet are relaxed. My arms are getting heavy. My feet are getting heavy. I just want to sleep. My eyes are relaxed. My eyes are getting very heavy. I want to fall asleep. I am beginning to fall asleep." Repeat these, or your own words, for up to five minutes. You may extend the repetition beyond five minutes at the beginning of your learning process. It takes practice for you to make your arm feel heavy, but later you will be able to make it feel heavy in one minute. Similar control can be learned for other parts of the body. The purpose is to induce relaxation. The heaviness occurs because the blood vessels in your arm have become relaxed, allowing more blood to flow into your arm.

Employing the principle of feedback helps to produce success in self-hypnosis as in all other activities. In order to do this, remember the suggestions that were most effective in bringing you into self-hypnosis. Write down these suggestions. Whatever worked best for you should be used again because it reveals the presence of a conditioned response already established in you. Other words and phrases that you may be responsive to are "contented, eyes are heavy, feelings are oozing away, everything is slowing down, I am floating and drifting." Some persons get better results with over-breathing and some do better with under-breathing. The feeling of warmth may take from four to ten minutes to produce even after you have learned the method. It is better all through your self-hypnosis process to keep an unhurried attitude.

There are no known examples of undesirable results coming from self-hypnosis of sane individuals. If you are a highly disturbed person, self-hypnosis without supervision might be counterproductive. No one stays in self-hypnosis long. You can get out of it if the telephone rings, taking a deep breath, saying that you feel fine or that you are wide awake. If you do not do anything at all to terminate the self-hypnosis, you will drift out of it naturally when you shift to another line of thought. You do not have to stay in self-hypnosis to reach the objective sought by your suggestions. Your subconscious mind will do that for you.

Experience has shown that the use of caffein drinks in the evening tends to interfere with self-hypnosis. A sense of fear with its accompanying tension will block the pathway to self-hypnosis. If you recognize a fear, you should examine yourself to find the source. When you find the source, you will realize the unreasonableness of continuing it. You can say to yourself that the reason for the fear is long gone and it will have no further effect on your subconscious mind. It may take several days to break the habitual thought pattern.

A fourth variation in the method of reaching self-hypnosis is to lie quietly as in the other methods, breathing rather deeply for a minute while focusing your eyes on a single spot. Close your eyes and count to ten at one count per second while concentrating on your right thumb. Continue doing the concentrating and counting for each of your fingers and your other thumb, keeping all other thoughts from interrupting. Finally count to ten with your eyes focused on an imaginary spot on your own forehead. By this time your mind should be drifting along in a state of self-hypnosis ready to receive suggestions. In order to relax more completely and go into a deeper level of self-hypnosis, tense your right arm a moment and let it go limp. At the same time try to have the rest of your body go limp. Then tense and let go your left arm, your right and left leg, your shoulders, your neck and face. As each group of muscles relaxes, you should be carried a little deeper while you are saying to yourself, "Now I am going deeper." Practice will improve your results. During this procedure, deeper than usual breathing may be helpful. Whenever you want to discontinue, you can use your own words or say, "Now I'm awake again." You will come out of it and feel refreshed. This method can also be used for short periods of daytime relaxation in a sitting position where sleep is not your objective. When you get into a deeper level of self-hypnosis, it is possible for you to take yourself back to last weekend, last Christmas, or to some other event. You can place yourself in the situation, living it over again word for word with the same sights and feelings.

The purpose of your self-hypnosis may be to change a habit pattern, such as smoking. If your true desire is not to stop smoking, your suggestion to your subconscious to stop smoking will slash with what your true desire is. In such a case, you have to reach your objective by indirection; first suggesting to yourself that smoking makes you nauseated or any suggestion that can turn your subconscious mind against smoking. When you have turned your true desire from smoking to not smoking, your suggestion to stop will succeed.

If you use self-hypnosis to reduce over-eating, you may have to reach your goal by suggesting numerous times that you wish to become slender. Your subconscious mind will become motivated to direct your activities toward the behavior characteristics that will produce slenderness. Other objectives you can achieve with your suggestions are deafness to particular annoying noises or partial anesthesia of a part of the body. It is better not to suggest general deafness to noise because you want to have your ears open to proper alarm signals. Care also should be used not to block out discomfort that is necessary to give you warning of a threat to your health. Neither the deafness or the anesthesia is lasting. Both have to be reinforced by new suggestions at frequent intervals. The sense of pain appears to be greatest in the skin. The flesh and organs are less sensitive to surgery than many persons believe. Some organs can be cut without pain.

A fifth method of producing self-hypnosis begins by assuming the previously described position in bed. Turn your head to the far right, hold an instant, then turn to the far left for an instant. Repeat ten times. Tense your neck and shoulders for an instant and let them go limp. Repeat ten times. Do the same with all the muscles of your right leg, lifting it a few inches off the bed. Then let it go limp. Repeat for the left leg. Follow the same procedure with each arm. Now you can start making suggestions to yourself to overcome habit patterns that prevent sleep. Say, "I am going to leave all my problems and troubles behind me. Shortly I will float off into sleep. Soon I will be asleep. I am going to sleep contentedly all night. I understand the reasons why I could not go to sleep in the past and they no longer apply to me." Continue with your selection of the above type of suggestion until it has taken effect.

In case you have been using sleeping pills say, "I will not need sleeping pills any more" or "Sleep will come easily to me without sleeping pills." If your habit is entrenched, reduce the dosage a little each night by shaving off part of the pills until you have none left. Repeat your suggestions for several minutes, once each time you breathe out. It will take several nights for your subconscious mind to reject sleeping pills. If you are truly addicted to them, it may take you much more time to reduce the dosage.

One individual states that after several months of patient practice, he can induce self-hypnosis by saying to himself each time he exhales, the word "drowsy." Reaching relaxation by means of self-hypnosis produces lasting change. When you go to bed, your attitude before and after lying down should be thankfulness for being able to drop all your problems until tomorrow. Change your habitual attitude from, "I cannot sleep" to "I can sleep." Start letting go as you prepare for bed. Look forward to feeling sleepy and floating away.

Whether it is reverie, daydream, meditation, autogenic suggestion, progressive relaxation, self-hypnosis or other methods leading to sleep: your eyes tend to focus on vacancy, sounds melt away into nothing and attention is diffused into a vague timelessness. This similarity of process argues for the contention that all of these states of entering sleep share a common approach to the brain. But it is self-hypnosis that can change your future.

Chapter XII

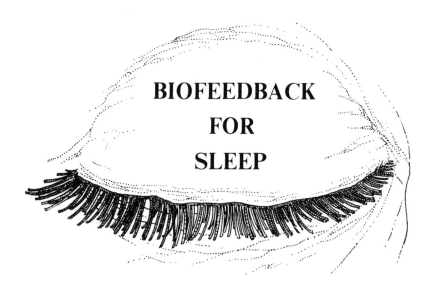

BIOFEEDBACK
FOR
SLEEP

Biofeedback is a new word for an old technique we have used every day since we were born. It is self-regulation and learning by observing the effect of whatever actions we take. It is learning by trial and error as we see, feel or hear the results of what we do. You learn to play ping pong by visual and muscular feedback. When you make a mistake, you correct your arm. If you do well, you try to repeat what you did. If you were blindfolded, the feedback would be cut off and your learning would stop. In learning to play the piano, you use feedback from feeling, hearing and seeing. As an infant you tried out all of your muscles in order to see and feel what effect their movement caused. The term is call biofeedback instead of feedback, because the word feedback in electronics, means the effect of a signal coming back to its point of origin to interfere with its continuance. It occurs when the microphone into which you are speaking receives your own amplified voice over the loudspeaker.

The biofeedback machines of today are the same as the electroencephalogram machines used for testing to examine the nature of sleep. The biofeedback machine must be adapted so that it is you who reads the results instead of the laboratory attendant in the next room. In biofeedback training, only one activity is measured at a time. Only the electrodes for that activity are attached to you. When you think, exercise your will or take an attitude, you can see, feel or hear what effect is produced.

Hopefully if you can see what is happening from light or sound signals, a line being drawn on a moving roll of graph paper or the needle on a dial, you can be trained to control the body function whose effect you are witnessing.

The procedure would be for you to go to one of the few medical laboratories or hospitals in the United States that have biofeedback machines, have a doctor or one of his staff attach you to the proper electrodes and start your training in learning to control what the doctor tells you need to control. The cost to you of all the professional personnel working on you, plus the cost of the office, plus the cost of your use of the $10,000 feedback machine would be prohibitive.

For measuring and learning the control of tension, the electrodes are attached to your forehead as a representative of all the muscle tension in your body. An alternative location for the electrodes is over the jaw muscles. You can read a dial or listen to the rate of clicks that indicate to you the level of your muscle tension. Tests show that for some persons, the use of the biofeedback machine increases muscular tension. If the training works for you, four to ten weeks of appointments should give you enough experience to perform without the biofeedback machine, coming back occasionally for a refresher test. Eventually you should be able to bring about the same relaxation at home that you would obtain with the help of the machine.

If your heartbeat is what you are going to learn to control, you will watch the measurement of your pulse as it is registered. You attempt by conscious effort to find an attitude that appears to reduce the rate of your heartbeat. Theoretically you could learn to do this by using your watch instead of a biofeedback machine. There are some who feel that attempting to learn voluntary control of a heartbeat is dangerous and should not be attempted.

If you want to learn to control your blood pressure, you would not be able to see what effect you are producing on yourself by exercise of your will or varieties of attitude. You can see by means of the biofeedback machine what effect your trial and error efforts have on your blood pressure. Eventually you learn which have the effect you want and how you can produce the attitude that causes this effect. You should be able to produce the attitude and the result without watching the biofeedback machine.

When the objective is to produce the alpha brain waves associated with the threshold of sleep and daydreams, the electrodes are attached to the scalp. An auditory signal comes on anytime you can make the brain waves as slow as the alpha rhythm. The sound goes off as soon as the brain waves are off that frequency, which is around seven to fourteen bursts per second. Those in the drug culture refer to the state of mind as the "alpha trip." Beta waves are those found during ordinary daytime activities at the rate of fourteen to forty bursts per second. Theta is four to seven cycles per second and is either sleep or the edge of sleep. Some meditators have claimed they cou'd reach theta, hold it, and think original world shaking thoughts. There is no scientific corroboration of such claims. One of the revelations of testing is that the alpha brain wave is attained more easily by those with low performance in school.

One experiment found that those who are taught to relax the muscles of the forehead, could bring themselves to sleep in twenty minutes. Generally self-training to go to sleep by means of the established non-machine methods can bring sleep more rapidly than that. The established methods of inducing sleep represent your own acquisition of a learned habit pattern rather than the temporary reaction to a machine. All authorities agree that the use of biofeedback machines requires supervision. Some authorities say that unsupervised use of the machine is as dangerous as the use of drugs.

There are biofeedback machines that range from $100 up to $10,000 in price. There is criticism of the low priced machines as not measuring accurately. Regulation of the sale and use of machines has been recommended. One manufacturer is quoted as suggesting that the machine should be restricted to use in a hospital or a doctor's office. Good machines constantly require skilled adjustment. Poor machines may not be adjustable or may not be worth the cost of adjustment. Those who use a biofeedback machine get either a disagreeable reaction or some benefit. In the latter case, the speed of learning varies greatly from person to person.

The use of the machine is very expensive and therefore limited in number of users. So far it is mainly a clinical health device. At the present time serious work continues in the field of biofeedback, little of it toward the goal of learning to go to sleep.

Chapter XIII

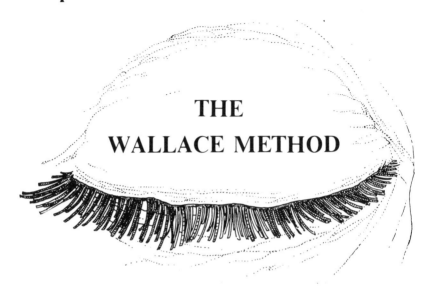

THE
WALLACE METHOD

J.M. Wallace was a faculty member of several colleges and universities. The focus of the Wallace method is on the relief of tension, much of which is below the level of consciousness. Individuals can be perpetually tense without knowing it. Wallace describes tension as physical and tangible. There is no such thing as nervous or mental tension, because the nerves and the brain are incapable of changing into tension. Only muscular fiber has the capacity to become tense or to contract.

Basically tension is due to the reaction of any organism to the instinct for self-preservation. The instinct goes into action automatically, but mistakenly, in most of our relations. Economic, social, familial, intellectual and physical problems set the instinct and thus tension into operation.

Wallace felt that tension interfered with much of life besides successful sleep. He charged tension with human relationship troubles, job and promotion loss, political, religious and racial antagonism and much of the violence about us.

He believed that if you knew how the body worked, you would have more of an incentive to do what was needed to make it work right. Those who learn how to make their bodies work look back on the past and ask themselves how they could have endured all their previous difficulties.

During tension adrenalin secretion is increased proportionally to tension, whether tension is caused by heavy labor, exercise or is non-moving chronic tension. In order to overcome tension so sleep may result, as well as an adjustment to the environment during the day, the skill of relaxation must be learned. This skill will bring sleep, increased self-confidence, better health and better appearance. Tension retards the repair of the tissues as well as the rate of healing. Susceptability to illness increases and the rate of recovery is slowed.

Wallace said that you can change your environment to get away from the alarms that are causing your tension. This may mean drastic changes in job, family, location or whatever may trigger your tension. You can also live by yourself without contact with other people. In some individuals, however, isolation itself produces tension. A third alternative is to take drugs or alcohol to slow down the brain and reduce the quantity of signals that reach it. This requires progressively larger amounts of alcohol or of drugs as tolerance develops in the cells of your body.

The fourth alternative available to you to eliminate the tension that retards your effectiveness and your sleep, is to learn the technique of relaxation into sleep. This enables you to adapt to your environment without any drastic changes and without giving up any of the accomplishments you have attained. The self-training can take a short or long time depending on whether you simply go through the motions or whether you concentrate and apply yourself.

The Wallace method is composed of nine lessons organized into ten steps of one week each. When the tenth week has passed, you should have acquired a lifelong technique for adapting yourself to your daily life and the needs of your brain and body in order to go to sleep easily. You will have learned a valuable skill which will enhance the performance of every other skill you possess.

Lie flat in bed, with a low pillow under your head, neck, and under your knees so that your legs are not straight and your thighs are raised. When the legs are straight and are in a line with your body, you are in a position that produces strain and tension. It is the position that often leads to a stiff back in the morning, and is often accompanied by a back ache. Your arms should be along your body with the elbows bent. The room should be quiet and dark. Your bladder should be empty.

Lie quietly a moment or two, then close your eyes. This will further reduce the flood of signals reaching your brain. Do nothing except concentrate on your breathing, noticing the rise and fall of your diaphragm. Breathe through your nose, noticing your exhalation and emphasizing it slightly. If your mind wanders from concentration on your breathing and diaphragm, bring it back without emotion. The purpose of this exercise is to have your chest and diaphragm relax. As they begin to let go, your breathing will become slower and deeper and all the muscles will tend to let go. From time to time you may take a deep breath. The concentration will be very poor on the beginning nights, but will slowly improve. Concentration on a single activity will, by itself, have a sleep inducing quality. Continue the same procedure for seven nights, reading this short instruction each night.

The second week is devoted to learning to relax the facial muscles. In preparation for turning your attention toward these muscles, spend about two minutes repeating lesson one. There is a close connection between the facial muscles and tension throughout the rest of your body. Nearly forty percent of the motor area of the brain which controls the muscles is taken up with the muscles of the face and throat. When the facial area of your brain is highly active, the carry over to the rest of your brain tends to increase tension in your whole body. The face is also important. More than any other area of the body, it reflects your emotional state.

Clench your jaw tightly for a moment and notice tension. Notice the feeling of relaxation when you let go. Repeat the clenching and relaxing twice, trying to notice the slightest tension in your jaw when it is relaxed.

Your tongue becomes tense because it gets little rest all day long. It is kept busy not only talking, but also unnecessarily vocalizing yout thoughts or talking to yourself. You often push your tongue against your teeth or pull it back into your throat which tenses your tongue and your throat. A relaxed tongue will not only improve the speed of relaxation for sleep, but will improve your voice.

For the second exercise push your tongue against the back of your front teeth, noticing the feeling of tension. Hold a moment and let your tongue go slowly and completely, noticing the feeling of limpness. Repeat this action once. Pull your tongue back as hard as you can. Notice the tension under the chin and over the front of the throat. Hold for a moment and let your tongue relax. Notice that the bottom of your chin and the front of the throat relax at the same time. Repeat once with less exertion. It is a good idea to check on the tension of your tongue from time to time all day.

It is important to recognize the forehead muscle called the *frontalis*, which is often in permanent tension. It causes the furrows in the forehead above your nose. It is a large flat muscle across the front of your head which, in combination with a similar muscle on the back part of your head, can put a squeeze on your entire scalp and produce a tension headache. Frown for a moment and let the frown go. Repeat the exercise once more, noticing that it screws up the muscles around the eyes at the same time. Let the muscle go. This muscle is used too often and contributes to tiredness and tension around your eyes. If this area is relaxed all day, it does not need to be trained to relax at night.

The smile muscles are often kept in a permanent fixed expression. At the end of the day there is tension in them and in the face and neck. A fixed grin causes the same kind of tension as the forehead frown. When your face is relaxed, it is difficult for you to be excited. To perform the smile exercise, smile hard for a moment. Be aware of the feeling of the muscles around the corners of your mouth, then let them go. After a few days, you will learn to be aware of the tension of these muscles and can discontinue it. Within a short time, you will begin to notice the improved appearance of your relaxed facial area.

The third week starts with a review of the exercises of the first two weeks. Then you will learn to relax your hands and arms. Your hands come after your face in reflecting agitation. As indicated before your hands are controlled by a disproportionately large area of your brain area. Tension results in constant motions of tapping, twisting, scratching, rubbing, clenching, twiddling or smoking. These movements are not only evidence of tension, but they tend to increase it. Perform the exercise by clenching your hand tight, noticing the feeling of tense muscles in your hand and forearm. You will be able to feel the tension from your clenched fist reach your upper arm and chest muscles. You can feel all the tension disappear just by unclenching your hand. With practice you will recognize the feeling of tension whenever it develops. When you can consciously keep your face and hand muscles in a relaxed state at all times, you will find that many daily problems no longer feel like problems and emotional equanimity replaces emotional disturbances. After a week of attention to your hands, the tension in your forearm and in the muscle between your thumb and first finger which often lingers on to the point of soreness after daytime activities, will be reduced.

Your fourth week is directed at relaxing the muscles of your neck. Learning neck relaxation is difficult. Your neck is at work nearly all the time that you are conscious. It becomes tense early in the day and remains so until sleep. Your neck muscles reflect every change in emotional level. As with other muscles that cause tension the muscles of your neck may be the source of pains and aches in your back, your head and your shoulders. Besides the tension that develops and the pains that may occur, you become fatigued sooner because nearly all muscles are in pairs, one pulling in one direction and the other pulling in the opposite direction. When your muscles are tense, it requires a greater mental impulse to get the muscles to move by tensing against the opposite partner.

To do the exercise, review the previous three weeks of exercises. Then press your head backward against your pillow for several seconds. Notice the sense of tension in your neck. Reduce the pressure slowly until relaxation is complete. Wait a minute and repeat less strongly. Many persons unconsciously lie in bed with their heads pressed against the pillow. Be aware that your neck muscles have let go and keep your mind on holding them limp. The second part of this exercise is to raise your shoulders as high as they will go for a moment, then let them go limp. Repeat this, noticing the feeling of tension and relaxation. Often you can see individuals going through the day with hunched or "chicken" shoulders. This places a strain on your neck and reduces the flow of blood.

Your fifth week of exercises is directed at your chest muscles and shoulder area. Shoulder tension is usually due to improper or unchanging posture. Your chest muscles tense in proportion to the state of your emotions. Tension can cause the arching of your pectoral muscles on the front of your chest. It causes the muscles between your ribs to tighten, making your breathing more difficult, more shallow and faster. Your diaphragm is your principal breathing muscle. Tension in the diaphragm increases the rate of your breathing. Consequently this reduces your physical capacity. The first part of this exercise is to place your finger tips together over your diaphragm. Take deep breaths, holding a few seconds and exhaling slowly while you pay attention to the relaxing of your muscles. Continue until you feel acquainted with the action of your muscles while you breathe. This will help avoid a constricted chest.

The second part of the fifth exercise is concerned with relaxing the large pectoral muscles across the front of your chest. They are used in all movements of your shoulders. Explore your left pectoral muscle with your hand, prodding it and moving it around to feel it when it is limp and when it is tense. Press your left arm to your side in order to feel the tension in your left pectoral muscle. Do the reverse for your right pectoral. Tension in the pectorals runs into the front muscles of your neck. After practicing awareness of tension in your pectorals, you will be able to recognize tension in them immediately and keep them relaxed unless they have work to do.

The third exercise of your fifth week is for the relaxation of the deltoid muscle in the side of your shoulder. This large muscle is used with most movements of your arms. It is fastened on either side in your back. Raise your right arm a few inches and feel your right deltoid with your left hand. Drop your arm and try to become aware of tension in your deltoid without using your hand to feel it. Then press your arm down toward the bed, again feeling the effect with your left hand. Next feel the effect without using your left hand. After exploring the tensing and relaxing of your right deltoid, repeat the same exercise by raising and pressing downward with your left arm. During the day your arms should hang loose without tension, instead of hanging at some angle or held out from your shoulder. Keep your shoulder limp except for the time when it is at work.

During the sixth week, you will learn to recognize and control tensions in your abdomen and your back. Many persons have a feeling of tightness in some region of the abdomen. You can have it below your sternum, at either side or simply have a general tight feeling. Usually this is not due to tension in muscles over which you have direct control. It is caused by muscles in your internal organs, called involuntary muscles. In order to control the tension in them, the excitement caused by the tension of many of your voluntary muscles has to be slowed and stopped. Tension in your face and hands has a direct effect on the tension in the internal organs. Your method of breathing also contributes to tension. To learn to control the voluntary muscles of your abdomen, continue the method of increasing tension until you are aware of it. Then recognize it and let go.

The exercise is performed by first reviewing the previous lessons. Then place your hands over your abdomen and press out with your abdomen. Hold a moment and let go. You will notice that you cannot breathe or cannot breathe easily with your abdomen tense. Repeat the exercise.

The second part of the exercise is to draw in your abdomen all the way, hold a moment and let it go. Notice again how your breathing is restricted as a result of this kind of tension. This tension is in a different group of muscles. If you learn to be aware of the tension in all of these muscles, you can relax them during the day and at night. Unnecessary tension in your abdomen does not mean that it is strong. Your abdomen ought to be strong for good health, posture and breathing.

The third exercise in this lesson applies to your back. Back tension is often called lumbago. A tense back injures more easily. It is the reason that back injuries are more frequent when you are worried, angry or concerned. Arch your back for several moments, noticing the feeling in your muscles. Then drop your back down. Repeat this movement arching only half as vigorously. Try to recognize the slightest amount of tension.

Lesson seven is for your legs and feet. It comes as a surprise to many persons that their legs and feet are a mirror of their tensions and emotions. This is shown by tapping, twisting, crossing, wiggling and curling them around the legs of your chair. As usual, start this week of lessons with a review of all the previous exercises. Raise your right leg several inches, keeping it straight. You will notice muscle tension in your abdomen and possibly in the small of your back. The muscles at the front and sides of your thigh will be hard if you feel them. Let your leg drop, feeling the lack of tension. Repeat the exercise, trying to remember the presence and absence of tension so you can eliminate leg tension when you feel it.

Your second leg exercise is to press the heel of your right leg into the bed to feel the muscle tension in the back of your thigh. You will notice tense muscles in your back and some tension in other parts of your leg. Repeat this exercise, observing that formerly you probably could lie flat in bed thinking that you were relaxed when, in fact, many of your muscles were tense.

The final two lessons are the most difficult. They are placed last in order to have the advantage of seven weeks of practice. Lesson eight is concerned with your muscles of speech. You may have noticed that you and other persons verbalize when you read, which not only slows the speed of reading, but is fatiguing. Verbalizing as you think is tension producing and tiring. There are forty-six muscles involved in speech. The activity they cause in the brain is great. We have previously considered how the high level of activity in your brain increases the tension to some extent in every muscle.

Start with a review of the previous exercises. Then put your fingertips on your throat just above your voice box and recite a saying or poem a few lines long. Notice your lips, your tongue and the feeling of movement in your throat. Try to recognize the spurts of tension in those muscles during speech. Relax for a few moments, then repeat the exercise. Concentrate on learning to recognize the feeling of the speech muscles when they are tense. Patience and repetition will be needed. This skill will be very helpful for getting to sleep.

Try to recite the same lines with your mouth closed. Notice that your lips, tongue and throat still move. If you can relax your muscles of speech, the level of your mental activity will fall. There is a theory that if you can totally relax your speech and eye muscles, conscious mental activity will stop and you will be asleep. With the passage of eight weeks, you have perceptibly or imperceptibly become a different person because of the gradual change that is taking place when you practice these exercises.

The ninth week will relax the muscles of your eyes. Visualization is part of mental activity. You have noticed that many people roll their eyes in various directions when they go through the thinking process. The thinking that requires visualization keeps the eye muscles in constant activity that is tiring and exhausting. More than any other activity, visualization increases mental excitement which raises the level of tension in all the muscles of your body, adding to your fatigue and possibly producing headaches.

Do a brief review of your previous lessons and close your eyes. Notice whether you can feel any tension in your eyes. Turn your eyes toward your left ear, hold a few seconds and let go. Remember the feeling of tension. Repeat the exercise by looking toward your right ear, feel the tension a few seconds and let go. Look up at your hairline for a moment and then let go. Then look down at your chin and let go. Each time note the feeling of tension. Whenever it occurs, you can try to stop it. Try visualizing a street scene of people and vehicles. Note that your eyes are constantly in motion as they sweep the parts of the scene into your mental image. In order to relax your eyes, you have to stop seeing images. In effect, you have to stop thinking. This is what happens to your eyes when you are falling asleep. The only substitute for non-visualization is to be able to concentrate solely on a black void. If you can do that, or if you can stop seeing images, you have begun to enter the stage of sleep.

Probably you have found some of the lessons more difficult than others, and some more helpful than others in getting to sleep. In time the difficult lessons will become easy and all of the lessons together will be a single fabric in which each one helps the others.

The only way that you can keep and improve the amount of skill you have acquired is to continue practicing the exercises. There is one further method called the tenth lesson. Apply the methods that you have learned lying in bed to other periods of the day. You can promote additional control over all tensions by doing the exercises for a few minutes each day in a sitting position. The objective is to apply the skills you have learned to everything that you do, using only the muscle tension needed to perform the acts you have to carry out during the day.

Chapter XIV

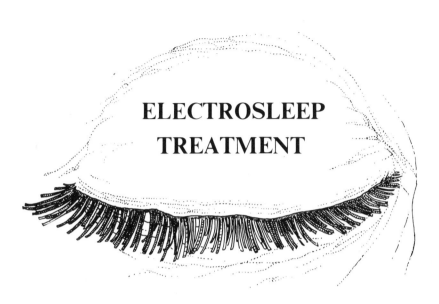

ELECTROSLEEP TREATMENT

Electrosleep treatment is not self-training for sleep. It is not capable of being used to train you for sleep. In fact the treatment is not usually given for the purpose of producing sleep. Electrosleep treatment is given in the laboratory for the purpose of producing electro-relaxation. The effect is caused by a tiny shock treatment. The subject matter is included here because to anyone hearing the name, the impression is given that a method of attaining sleep is being described.

For many years health treatment in a small number of Russian clinics has offered this modified shock treatment. It is so mild that it does not hurt. The electric current is applied through electrodes attached to the head of the patient so that some change is made in the electric charge of the cells of the brain. Generally patients come away from the treatment with a sense of relaxation. Much of the treatment is used for treating depression and agitation. There has been experimentation in Europe and Israel more than in North America. Experiments in these countries show a wide variety of reactions to treatment. For some individuals there is no improvement of tension.

The reports from Russia claim that the mental illnesses of

most persons may be improved for months. The Russians call their method "Electroson." They refer to the method as an electric tranquilizer and theorize that the current permits the re-establishment of normal brain rhythms when those rhythms have become desynchronized. Persons in depression may have irregular stages of sleep with the stages shifting out of proper sequence. For those with some kind of mental unbalance, the sleep cycle that ordinarily is a rigid ninety minutes contains no particular length.

The electrosleep treatment has been tried to a limited extent in the United States. Doctors in the United States and in England have not recognized the claims from Russian clinics about the advantages that can be obtained through electrosleep treatment. The treatment does have a placebo effect on the patient. He feels the way he thinks he is supposed to feel in response to the treatment. There is little doubt remaining, however, that the electrosleep treatment does quiet psychiatric patients and children who are having tantrums. One American experimenter says that it is not known what is happening when the electrosleep treatment is administered.

When used for the purpose of inducing sleep, the electric treatment does not promote sleep in all persons. For those who do go to sleep when connected to the electrodes of the electro-sleep equipment, there is no after-effect on the quality of sleep out of the laboratory. One generally widespread reaction to the treatment in healthy persons is a feeling of being refreshed. Some persons describe it as feeling as if they had had some sleep. Some simply stay drowsy and never feel refreshed. Patients do come out of the treatment with a greater feeling of detachment and a passive attitude. In an American experiment conducted over a period of time with many hundreds of patients, sixty percent of persons treated felt some improvement in their tension.

The prediction is that electrosleep will be used more often in North America in hospitals and clinics as an alternative type of treatment. However, electrosleep gets its effect without any self-direction or self-training on the part of the patient.

Chapter XV

ZEN MEDITATION
FOR SLEEP

It is claimed that the meditating state of Zen is a good prelude for sleep. There is no reason why the practice of Zen could not be moved from the floor to your bed and practiced there in order to bring on sleep.

Followers of Zen look upon the emotional state they seek to promote and carry out through the day as the important objective. It will enable the easy entry into sleep separate from the period of actual Zen meditation. When the Zen meditator approaches the time for sleep, he should not have to prepare himself because he does not have to discard the emotions and tensions accumulated during the day.

No philosophical or religious dogma is required in order to practice Zen meditation, although individual teachers of Zen may have a variety of personal dogma. Zen arose centuries ago as a refinement of Buddhism but, the meditation does not have to be religious in character any more than western meditation has to be Christian in character.

Your objective in Zen meditation is an inner harmony. It should eliminate personal doubts and uncertainties, depression, agitation and fear. You are seeking to acquire a sense of detachment and self-control. You will learn more about yourself. Serious practitioners, devoting considerable time to meditation, seek an undefinable enlightenment or a type of joy and freedom from concern, sometimes described as a sense of oneness with nature. In Japanese this state is called "satori."

You can learn and practice Zen by yourself, although it is easier and quicker if you have a master to instruct and encourage you. The teacher refers to himself as a master. A master's directions to you are usually very few, seemingly vague and may appear to be irrelevant. As a student, you are really left to learn almost entirely through your own experience. Whatever you get out of the meditation is an experience that is personal to you. It is not the same as anyone else's experience. After the master starts you out in the proper form, there will be little for him to do except to encourage you to continue.

The recommended setting for doing Zen meditation is an area on the floor 3' by 5' opposite a blank section of wall in a quiet place. Orthodox Zen is performed in a sitting position on a very thick cushion facing the blank section of wall. Your legs are in the "lotus" position with the top of each foot turned upside down and resting on the top of the opposite thigh. For most Americans this position is so painful that after a few minutes meditation would be impossible. Some persons cannot even get their legs into the lotus position. An alternative is the "half lotus" position in which you put one foot upside down resting on top of the opposite thigh, and the other foot under the crotch. A third alternative position starts by kneeling and then graduates to sitting on your heels. In this position your lower legs go to sleep and become numb. The discomfort may interfere with the possibility of successful meditation. A fourth approved position is to sit on the edge of a cushioned stool six or eight inches high with your legs folded in front of you. The goal is to have your back held straight, head erect, hands folded and resting in your lap with the palms up. The idea is to have a sitting position in which there is an easy balance without exerting your front, back or side muscles in order to keep your balance. There are quasi-religious ideas about the advantages of the described position in order to meditate. A fifth position, used for going to sleep only, is to lie in bed with low pillows under your head and neck, a cushion or support under your knees and your arms at your sides.

Once you are in position, no movement is made except for breathing. Focus your eyes on a real or imaginary spot directly opposite to your face during the whole period of your meditation. At the beginning, this will last for twenty minutes. The period should not start until one hour after eating a meal in order to avoid drowsiness and sleep. A good time is immediately before breakfast.

When you have assumed the position, start counting mentally from one to ten. Count one for each long inhalation. For the exhalation you can use the word "and" between numerical counts if you like. Concentrate your mind entirely on your counting. Drive out any interrupting thoughts. You will find such concentration impossible at the beginning, but that is what meditation is all about. Day by day and month by month, the ability to concentrate on counting to the exclusion of all other thoughts will slowly improve. Continuous holding of attention is contrary to usual human behavior. When you can control your thoughts you will have true self-control. What you think is what you are. What you think about is what you will be. Counting with your eyes closed is permissible in order to aid in the concentration.

After two weeks of daily twenty minute sessions concentrating solely on your slow breathing, it should become as automatic as a conditioned reaction. The counting can now be stopped. In place of counting, continue your long, slow breathing automatically. Concentrate on the word "nothingness." Exclude all thoughts except your concentration on nothingness.

The Japanese word for nothingness is "mu." Some teachers recommend it. You may use it if you wish, provided that you treat it as a word with the same meaning as nothingness. The word nothingness should really carry more meaning to you than the word mu. Try to locate the sense of nothingness inside your abdomen. Continue to empty your mind of all other thoughts. Utter the word to yourself under your breath or say it aloud with great self-exhortation in order to attain a state of total concentration on nothingness.

At the end of twenty minutes of such concentration and self-exhortation, get up and move around. If possible keep the concept of nothingness with you all day long. If you can fit in another twenty minute period of meditation each day, the sense of relaxation, self control, freedom from agitation and inner harmony will become yours sooner. When you have learned the routine described here, you may step up to a forty minute period of meditation for greater results.

In Japan there are Zen retreats for continuous meditations for five to seven days, which may be likened to a crash course in Zen meditation. Many individuals have started such a self-training course. Not all persisted for five or seven days, but any meditation for more than one day is a type of crash course. If you do consider such a self-training course, the procedure for you to follow is the same as that used in the Japanese five day courses which is similar to the following pattern:

The day is divided into nine periods for meditation, each consisting of forty minutes of meditation and twenty minutes of walking very slowly and resting. The first period of meditation is the hour before breakfast. For one hour after breakfast you may rest or take care of your other activities. Then you start the first of three successive periods of forty minutes of meditation followed by twenty minutes of slowly walking or resting. Do not get out of the mood. Lunch is next followed by an hour of rest or other needed activities. Three successive periods of meditation are then carried out exactly the same as during the morning. The evening meal is followed by an hour of rest or other activities. Then there are two more successive periods of meditation. It is permissible to nap after meals. One of the principal problems is to stay awake. In a professional retreat several meditators are lined up along a wall and more face the opposite wall. A watchman observes the meditators to see that they do not deviate from the set procedure, and do not go to sleep. From time to time he will strike each meditator across the shoulders with a whip to keep him from falling asleep.

By the end of the fifth day, everyone moves more slowly. The sensations and experiences of each person are different. Some may even have a type of hallucination. The general result of the whole experience is a definite improvement in the ability to concentrate on one thing at a time without interruptions from other trains of thought. Further advantages are a sense of harmony, greater self-control, relief from tension and a feeling of accomplishment. One of the results of the orthodox Zen meditation is a removal of the attitudes and emotions that blocked the easy entry into sleep. The fifth position for using Zen as a technique for overcoming sleeplessness, should start to produce successful results almost from the first night.

Lie flat with your eyes closed and fixed on a single imaginary point in front of you. Start the concentration counting slow deep breaths from one to ten, excluding all other thoughts as far as possible. After following this simple procedure rigidly for two weeks, you may stop counting and turn your concentration to nothingness. If nothingness works for you, you may continue it. If not, go back to the more tangible concentration, counting from one to ten until sleep overtakes you. With practice, sleep will come more and more quickly and will bring you pleasanter and more productive days.

Chapter XVI

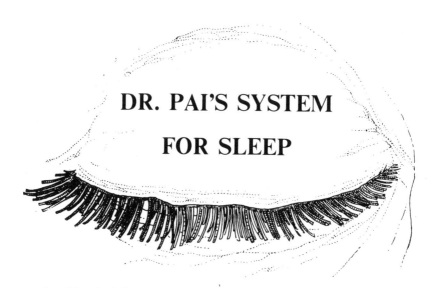

DR. PAI'S SYSTEM

FOR SLEEP

Dr. N. M. Pai got his experience in England in assignments in the National Health Program which were related, in some periods, especially to sleep problems. He introduces his system with one of the earliest exhortations from a physician against the use of sleeping pills. He outlines the damage they do to the quality of sleep and the rapid development of tolerance to them. He cites statistics about accidental and intentional death from pills as well as the kinds of poisoning they can cause.

According to Pai, the fear of not being able to go to sleep is what blocks sleep. In many cases, insomnia can be controlled by regular sleeping hours, a dark room and lying quietly. You may also try getting up for a while to read the dictionary, try writing your autobiography, or think about daily events during childhood. The persons who do not succeed with these simple measures need a relaxation technique.

Dr. Pai has more than one technique to recommend. For those who cannot get to sleep, he recommends the "tenlax" method which combats anxiety that prevents the frame of mind required to turn your brain to sleep. He says that in modern society you should convince yourself that there is no real reason for anxiety.

He suggests lying comfortably on your back, eyes closed, in a dark quiet room. He believes your bedroom should be green in color. Even the window shades should be green because it is relaxing and comforting to your eyes. Next tense your muscles by stretching your legs, pointing your toes away from you. Tense your legs as hard as you can for as long as you can, pressing the backs downward. Let go suddenly. Wait a moment and repeat, doing six maximum leg tensings. Tense the muscles of your arms and clench your fists as tightly as you can. Hold for as long as you can without discomfort. Then let go suddenly. Repeat this exercise a total of six times. With your eyes still closed, focus on the end of your nose for a moment, then focus on your hairline. If you feel like stopping the foregoing process at any point in order to sink into sleep, do so.

More severe insomnia may be treated with another process. When anxiety or fear is at a high enough level, your thoughts run on in a fever of activity and repetition, showing great activity in your brain. When your brain is feverishly active, it shows up in muscle tension, higher pulse and breathing rate, stomach discomfort, possible tremor and sweating on your hands and in your armpits. It is as if you are in mortal danger because you have given your brain the signal that your defense system must be aroused. First persuade yourself that you are not in mortal danger. Then follow the deep breathing process.

Focus your eyes on the end of your nose and hold them steadily in that position during the entire exercise. Hold your nose between your thumb and little finger. Press your right nostril closed and breathe in long and deeply through your left nostril. Hold your breath as long as you can. Then breathe out through your right nostril, closing the left with your finger. Continue to focus your eyes on the end of your nose. Part of the success of this exercise is due to your breathing and part to your concentration on what you are doing. Continue to do the alternate nostril breathing exercise until your tension and anxiety are relieved, you become drowsy, your eyes feel like turning upward into the eye position for sleep and you actually do sink into sleep.

Dr. Pai describes a further method of getting to sleep which was directed to those who have been using sleeping pills and have completed withdrawal from them. Such persons need to regain their self-confidence as well as free themselves from the use of sleeping pills.

Because the level of brain activity is so dependent on the amount of stimulating signals it is receiving from your senses, it is important to cut off light to stop visual stimulation to your brain. This tends to increase awareness to sound. Sound needs to be eliminated as much as possible. If it cannot be reduced sufficiently, soft music can be used to mask out the sound. For this method, the setting and position are the same. Again hold your nostrils, closing one to breathe in and closing the other to exhale, using long, slow breaths. While continuing your nostril breathing, tense your leg muscles, point your toes and lift your tensed legs slightly. Hold your leg tension as long as you can. Then let your muscles go and drop your legs. Discontinue your nostril breathing and tense the muscles of your arms hard. Clench your fists, hold for twenty seconds and let go. Wait a half minute after each exercise. Raise your head and shoulders just off your bed and hold for about twenty seconds, then let go. Stretch your right leg, pointing your toes. Tense the whole leg while you hold it off the bed for fifteen seconds or more. Let all your muscles go and let your leg drop. Repeat this exercise with alternate legs four times. Clench your fists, bend your elbows completely, tense the muscles of your arm hard and hold as long as you can whild holding your breath. Then let go. Breathe deeply and lie wholly relaxed. Stop doing the foregoing exercises any time you feel you are near to falling asleep. Lie back fully relaxed, turn your eyes upward and drop off to sleep. Dr. Pai believed that his system of exercises gave many of his 4,000 patients good sleep after relatively few lessons.

For those who wake up during the night and have mid-sleep insomnia, he also suggests eating less starchy food in the evening. Such food may ferment, producing gas and stomach discomfort. It may help to drink milk. You may eat a cracker to soothe your stomach. Caffeine drinks before going to bed may also cause mid-sleep awakening.

For those who awaken early in the morning after a good night's sleep, try the exercises. If they do not work, you probably have had all the sleep you need.

Chapter XVII

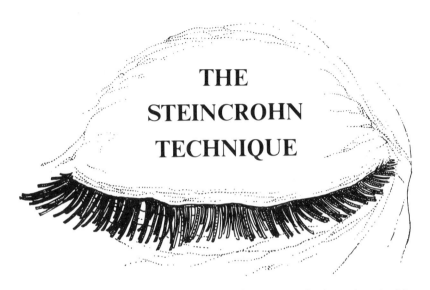

THE STEINCROHN TECHNIQUE

Rather than originating a technique, Dr. Steincrohn, in his medical practice, drew on what would be called the tried and tested methods for getting good sleep. He demonstrated a sympathy and understanding of the person who seeks to get the sleep he needs. He mentions that the subject most commented on after the weather is sleep. Sleep relates to many important parts of your existence. These include fatigue, slow reflexes, irritability, lack of ambition, enthusiasm and energy, lack of attractiveness, an inability to succeed and a shortened life span. Other items on the list include inefficiency on the job, accidents at home, on the highway and at work and a tendency toward illness.

The Steincrohn technique promotes lack of concern about going to sleep. Never try hard to go to sleep. Those who act as if they do not care about going to sleep find sleep effortlessly. Trying too hard creates anxiety which prevents the chemistry that permits sleep. The onset of sleep is also affected by resentment, jealousy, unreturned affection, business and family dissatisfactions, fear of illness, or breathing problems. Fatigue is almost always due to loss of sleep rather than to work, exercise, diet or illness.

Although everyone has his own sleep requirement, just lying

in bed without being asleep will do you about seventy-five percent as much good as if you had been asleep. However, the benefits of sleep are so great that the struggle to create the proper conditions for sleep are worthwhile.

You should lie on your back, arms at sides, using pillows under your head, neck and knees for a comfortable position. Sleep on a firm mattress. Try to be in a quiet, dark room or else place a black cloth over your eyes and plug your ears. Steincrohn advocates the Jacobson method which also permits lying on your side. First clench your right fist, raising it off the bed with all the muscles tense for one minute. Then let your arm go limp, dropping it to the bed. After a minute repeat the arm and fist tension, but let the tension relax slowly as your body relaxes too. Do the exercise once more, letting the tension decrease very gradually until your arm is totally limp.

Second, push both toes downward as far as they will go and hold there one minute. Stop the tension suddenly. Repeat the exercise relaxing slowly. In a moment repeat again, letting your tension decrease very gradually.

Third, relax your chest by breathing in more deeply than usual; hold your breath a moment; then let your chest go limp. Repeat this several times and try to relax the muscles of your chest.

The fourth exercise is for your forehead and face. Your forehead muscle is one of the general tests for body tension. Raise your forehead for a moment, then let it relax slowly. Repeat twice. Squeeze your forehead into a frown and gradually relax it, trying to attain a general relaxation. Repeat twice.

The fifth exercise is for your eyes. Start looking as far as you can toward your right ear for a half minute, then let your eyes go free. After a moment of relaxation, do the same exercise looking as far as you can toward your left ear for half a minute, then let your eyes go free. Next look up toward your hairline for half a minute before relaxing your eyes. Finally look toward your chin for a half a minute before letting go. Try to obtain general relaxation over your entire body each time your relax a set of muscles in the exercises. Try to remember the feeling of tension in the tightened muscles in each exercise as well as the feeling of relaxation when the muscle tension is gone. Whenever you feel such tension, during the day or before going to sleep, you can direct the muscles to relax.

Your sixth exercise is to learn to relax the muscles of your speech area. Count audibly to ten, noticing the tension required in the muscles of your throat, lips, tongue and face. Seek to relax all those muscles. Repeat this exercise counting to ten with less and less muscle movement and volume. Try not to use your muscles of speech at all. The performing of these exercises each night eventually allows you to trigger all of the relaxation exercises in a moment, so your brain gets the signal of relaxation and then gives the signal for sleep. Practice should be carried out faithfully every night in order to learn the skill.

Other aids to the technique of getting to sleep are offered. Steincrohn suggests imagining you are watching a swinging pendulum until your eyes become relaxed and your mind dulls. If this results in sleep, no further exercise is needed. If not, roll your eyes in figure eights, or circles until they are tired. Another exercise is to inhale deeply, hold your breath ten seconds and exhale slowly several times. Finally try counting your breaths from one to one hundred. If you last that long, count back from one hundred to one. You may also concentrate on your diaphragm during the counting. Try imagining that your arm is so heavy that you cannot lift it. Try it with your leg, both arms and both legs.

Steincrohn does not dismiss individual sleep techniques developed by you if they work. Whatever works should be used. Some of the following techniques that have worked for some individuals may work for you. A smile on your face brings sleep quicker than a frown. Acceptance of the world and cheerfulness help bring sleep. An ounce of wine before going to bed is sleep inducing for some. It is better to be covered. Excessive salt in the diet may delay sleep. Smoking before going to bed slows the coming of sleep. Cat-nappers fall asleep more easily at night. Try putting the mattress on the floor or reversing the head and foot of the bed. Name all the cities beginning with the letter "A" and then "B" and so on. Do the same with flowers. Read something monotonous just before going to sleep. Sleep alone. Use a fan or other soothing noise maker. Cover your eyes with something black. Go to bed at the same hour every night. Avoid drinking coffee or tea for supper and later at night. Repeat the same poetry or word jingle every night. Think loose.

Chapter XVIII

YOGA METHODS

The practice of yoga has hundreds of approaches, each to fit one of the hundreds of sects in India. The western adaptations are many, some with and some without religious dogma, some using Hindu words instead of the English equivalents. Specific relaxation techniques have been arranged for the purpose of approaching sleep. As with other relaxation techniques, yoga is intended primarily for controlling or eliminating the tensions, emotions, envies, anxieties and hostilities of the daytime.

Some teachers advocate five minute yoga sessions, some ten minute sessions and some advocate a session every time you have an outbreak of anger, fear, jealousy or frustration. The ultimate yoga goal is to do away with useless thoughts, fantasies and lack of attention so that you can concentrate better, avoid emotion and feel tranquil. You will thus find an easy entry into sleep.

Begin by lying in bed flat on your back, with or without pillows according to your own comfort. Close your eyes and keep your arms at your sides. You may also place one hand on your diaphragm in order to feel your breathing. Slow down the activity of your mind. Try to blank our all conscious thought, concentrating on one pleasant thought. Bring your mind back to that one thought each time it wanders away.

The exercise consists of breathing in through your nose slowly and filling your lungs to the count of five. Hold for a count of five and exhale to the count of five. Move only your diaphragm without raising of lowering your chest. One variation is to use your own pulse in order to time your breathing. With your finger on your pulse, inhale for eight beats, hold for four beats, exhale for eight beats and hold for four beats. Longer counts can be used. Once a rhythm of breathing is established, point your eyes upward toward your forehead and hold them there until uncomfortable. Hold them down for the same amount of time, then hold them right and left for equal amounts of time. Turn your eyes in a circle several times one way and several times the other way. Continuously look forward to sleep.

The remainder of this particular technique applies the principle of tensing and letting go of single groups of muscles. First concentrate on stretching and tensing your toes to the count of ten. Then relax your toes. Tense and clench your toes to your feet to the count of ten and relax them. Tense your calves and your thighs to the count of ten and relax. Continue this pattern by tensing and relaxing the muscles of your abdomen, chest, arms, hands, neck, face, jaw, tongue, forehead and lips. At one point or another you will sink into sleep; your eyes will roll upward, your brain will be blank.

Another variation is as follows: Lie in bed, raise your right arm straight above your head in line with your body, stretch your right side from toes to fingers as far as you can, noticing the feeling and release. After a moment repeat the same stretch and release on your left side. This is to start the process of relaxation. Next stretch your neck so that the nape feels stretched. Pull in your chin. This is close to the proper position for holding your head and neck. Then let go. Now put your palms on top of your head and pull backwards for half a minute. Stretch your face and let go. Your face will have lost tension. Yawn with your mouth wide open several times. Hold your tongue against the side of your cheek for ten seconds and release. Bug your eyes out for ten seconds and relax them. Massage each finger and thumb, then shake your hands up, down and sideways. Bend your arm double over your chest, clench your fist hard and tense your whole arm. Then relax. Repeat two or three times. Do the same exercise with your left arm. Press your legs against each other hard, pulling your toes toward you for a minute or more and relax. Repeat until you feel no tension in your legs. Expand your chest as much as possible, hold for a few seconds and exhale slowly. Repeat several times until you feel that your chest is relaxed. Try exhaling and pulling in your stomach toward your back bone as far as possible, hold a few seconds and let go. Repeat this several times to remove the tension from your abdomen. Yawn one or more times. At some point you will have floated into sleep.

One of the simplest yoga methods of reaching sleep is a combination of breathing and meditation. In this method, you lie in bed in the best position for you, using pillows or supports for your neck, knees and elbows. Keep your eyes closed. You should be in a dark, quiet room. Start by stretching as far as you can with your right leg and arm; then with your left leg and arm. Stretch your neck by turning your head to your right, pulling in your chin and stretching the left side of your neck behind your left ear. Do the same exercise turning your head to your left. After you have finished stretching your body in these ways, start taking slow, deep, full breaths. You may hasten the slowdown of all your body processes and promote relaxation by taking your deep breaths in through one nostril and out through the other. Meanwhile give directions to your eyes to feel heavy. During your breathing you may rest one hand on your diaphragm. Now you are ready for the meditation by counting your breaths from one to ten. Concentrate only on the counting, gently bringing your mind back every time it wanders. It will be wandering almost all of the time and you will be bringing it back to counting constantly. With practice your meditation will extend the length of the periods you can concentrate. At some point you will sink into the serenity of sleep.

Every night of practice will produce a cumulative effect in your ability to concentrate on counting your breaths up to ten. Such a change in your ability to concentrate will slow down your mind. You will find some carry over of the ability to concentrate in your daily activities. Your days will feel more relaxed. You will have a greater sense of control over yourself and your environment and greater peace of mind.

Your concentration does not have to be on counting your breath. It is a favored method because it is active and tangible. You can concentrate on breathing without counting or on your pulse rate. You can also concentrate on a mantra which means a sacred word in Hindustani. Ordinarily, in the west, it is the word you or someone else chooses for you. It can be the word for one night of meditation or used permanently. The word "butterfly" could be a mantra. One of the popular words is "om." Its devotees claim that the sound of it massages your insides and relaxes your muscles and tensions.

It is important not to be impatient or irritated by the wandering of your mind from the focus of your concentration. Generally it is true that you cannot stop your mind from moving from thought to thought, but you can gradually learn to reduce the wandering. One of the important activities in the meditative phase of the yoga system is that it causes the distracting thoughts to be pleasant and positive ones. In yoga, as in other methods, it cannot be over-emphasized that at bedtime, your brain and the state of your mind is a reflection of the state of your muscles. Every tense muscle increases the activity of your brain when you want to go to sleep. In yoga as well as in most other systems, an effective way to reduce tension is to tense a muscle group and then release it. This simple procedure causes the voluntary as well as the involuntary tension to disappear.

Chapter XIX

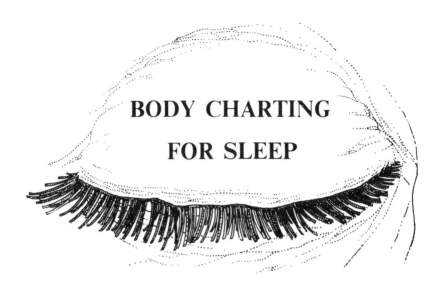

BODY CHARTING
FOR SLEEP

It is interesting that most of us know little about the information that our bodies can give to us. The rhythms that are going on in us are many. Most of them are unknown to us. Some have a direct effect on the ease with which we go to sleep as well as the kind of sleep we get. They may have an effect on the amount of sleep we need. There is no way you can find out about your own body rhythms except by discovering them by means of a record maintained for a minimum of thirty days to ninety days. The record you make will reveal information to you that you can utilize for other purposes besides sleep. Your cycles of mood, energy, appetites and effectiveness will furnish you with information on how to get the most out of your days.

The rhythms within us perform with a dependable cadence throughout our lives. Sometime during the remote past, each rhythm was molded into the master blueprint that governs our make-up and our body processes. Most rhythms arose for some reasonable purpose to promote survival. Some date back to progenitors associated with the sea, and are related to the movements of the moon and tides. Some are triggered by light and darkness. Light affects other types of cells in the body besides those of the optic nerves.

Some descriptions of our body rhythms refer to them as internal time clocks that set off reactions within us. They tell us when to sleep, when to awaken, when to feel hungry or thirsty, when to exercise, when to rest, when to seek company or solitude, when to feel exhilarated and when to feel lethargic. These rhythms affect our attitudes, energy, attention, digestion, breathing, pulse, alertness, health and our sleep.

A few of these rhythmic cycles include the ninety minute cycles of sleep, the apparent ninety minute cycle of increased hunger, the daily cycles of increased alertness, the nightly lowermost point of body processes around three to five o'clock in the morning and the onset and subsidence of oestrus in the reproductive cycle.

Most of us go about our daily affairs as if most of these cycles do not exist. We become frustrated because our activities are in conflict with basic rhythmic cycles that tend to block what we try to do. If we can discover what the more important cycles are and when they may be expected to rise and fall, we can harness or cooperate with them to aid our objectives. We can use such knowledge of our internal cycles to assist us in learning to sleep successfully.

After you have maintained your body chart record for a long enough period, you will develop a new respect for the complexity and wonder of the body you inhabit. Some persons have kept their body chart for many years until they have memorized it. Some persons have lived in tune with themselves for decades, multiplying their effectiveness, their usefulness and their joy of living.

The following items are a suggested list for body charting. You can make your own list on a single sheet of paper and duplicate it. Run perpendicular lines down your sheet of paper so that there is a column for each day. Perhaps you can get a week on each sheet of your record. After a month or more, you will want to prepare a line chart on a sheet of graph paper for some of your rhythms in order to show the ups and downs over a period of a month.

1. Hour of going to bed
2. Time taken to go to sleep
3. Quality of sleep
4. Hour of awakening
5. Naps during the day
6. Snacks before retiring
7. Beverages during the evening
8. Alcohol during the evening
9. Amount of exercise; type
10. Level of energy
11. Appetite
12. Diet
13. Weight upon arising
14. Elimination
15. Pains; discomforts
16. Smoking
17. Sexual activity
18. Exhilaration
19. Depression
20. Alertness
21. Dullness
22. Tenseness
23. Relaxation
24. Energetic periods
25. Lethargic periods
26. Desire to be sociable
27. Withdrawal
28. Clumsiness
29. Coordination
30. Unusual events

Chapter XX

SLEEP EQUIPMENT

Sleep equipment includes all the paraphernalia that can be related to the period of sleep. Bedding should be the weight you prefer. Your own bed clothes need to be made of the material that you find most comfortable. Your bed should be agreeably firm. Pillows can be any shape or size, but should be capable of keeping your head a little more than one inch above the mattress when you are lying on your back. They should allow your head to be relatively straight with your spine when you are lying on your side.

There are a few sleep shops, mostly in the very largest cities, which offer many sleep gadgets. If these items help you to hypnotize yourself into sleep, they may be worth having, but ultimately the state that brings sleep must come from within yourself. There are beds that vibrate or vibrators that vibrate your bed or mattress. A few individuals recommend water beds for sleep. Some persons prefer no bed under their mattress. Some believe you must be in tune with the lines of magnetic force between the north and south poles. The majority of advisors are firmly in favor of sleeping alone in your own room or at least sleeping in a separate bed. There is a variety of exercise equipment which tires and relaxes before bed.

Food for sleep might be included in the list of sleep equipment. Milk is the most frequent item listed because it is partly a protein food containing amino acids that break down into serotonin. Serotonin is one of the chemicals which induces sleep in the brain. Soft, bland food such as rice, bread or crackers comfort, relax and draw blood to the stomach from the rest of the body.

One of the more essential classes of equipment relates to the eyes and the ears. If your room does not get dark, you can cover your eyes with anything that stops light from reaching them, such as a sock, a handkerchief or a length of dark, soft cloth. This should be up to twenty-four inches long and reach around your head and neck far enought to remain in place all night. Professional eye covers are only needed for sleeping in a sitting position.

Noise may be reduced by any kind of ear plugs you can fashion. Soft wax soaked into cotton is the usual commercial ear plug. It can be bought at a drugstore. The optimum size of waxed cotton is the circumference of a penny and the thickness of a half dollar. Such a plug will last for many nights if touched with vaseline each evening. The other method of reducing the effect of noise is to create steady sound to blank out the disturbing noises. This may be done with an electric fan, an air conditioner or soft music. Even a program of continuous news repeated every few minutes can be used. Commercial "white noise" makers or recordings have been used to produce this result. Many individuals have solved their sleep equipment problems with materials of their own.

Chapter XXI

AUTHOR'S COMMENTS

I have followed all the sleep methods described herein for various periods, always with some success. I followed none of them for over a year except the Jacobson method number two and the Kelly method. They were first available when my interest and need arose many years ago. For a long time there was nothing to compare with the Jacobson method. If I were starting to learn one of the techniques today, I might conclude that the Jacobson method takes longer to yield results. I learned the Jacobson method so thoroughly that I could achieve the habitual response to the tense and relax system by an abbreviated form. I would simply tense my right little finger upward for a moment and let all muscles collapse limp when I let it drop. If I happened to be more agitated at bedtime, I raised my whole hand or my whole hand and my toes for a moment in order to trigger the release of all the muscles.

When I learned that there was a Kelly method of breathing into sleep, I continued the Jacobson hand and toe tensing during the inhaling. The letting go was done upon exhalation. I found immediate success with the first trial of the Kelly breathing method. The great advantage of the Kelly system is that the learning process is very short. For me, the Kelly method worked better during mid-sleep awakening than the Jacobson method alone. I sometimes combined the Kelly method with the use of a mantra and a self-suggestion while exhaling, especially if I came to bed overwrought. This worked very well for me.

I have also tried using the word "void" upon inhaling and the phrase "contentedly calm" during exhalation, which violates the rule that only one suggestion should be used at a time. I am not sure that any advantage arose out of using two suggestions at the same time. I felt that the Kelly technique of looking upward and seeing nothing but black during the breathing was excellent. It has occasionally been repeated in later techniques as a method of hastening relaxation. Seeing black does at least two things. It quiets the muscles of the eye and it reduces the activity of the brain by eliminating visual images. Both events reduce residual tension throughout the body. I have used the practice of seeing black while looking upward several times each day. I usually put my elbows on my knees, or on the desk and my palms over my eyes. I do this for a few seconds or for as much as two minutes. It always slows down the agitation from my activities to a more comfortable level.

Another aid that I learned from Kelly was loss of concern for fresh air. He demonstrated that two people cannot use up enough of the air in a closed bedroom in one night for the body to notice the difference. Ben Franklin, who could not sleep with a closed window, had to share a bedroom with a man who could not sleep with an open window. Franklin prevailed and the shutters were pushed open. Franklin slept perfectly, but the other man did not get a wink. In the morning they discovered that the shutters they pushed back opened onto a small closet.

The next sleep technique I tried to learn was meditation. There are several types of meditation, but at that time I was only acquainted with the mantra or word type. I used "void," "ah" and "om" for the words. I found meaningless words less productive than the later technique of self-suggestion ideas. I also found that, for me, meditation did not overcome agitation enough to sleep. I think I may have concentrated too hard and thus created tension instead of relieving it. I felt that meditation for sleep needed to start with some degree of placidity. I may not have given it the time to learn it well.

Zen next gained my attention. In my Zen experience, I found the nothingness concept somewhat related to the voidness attitude I had first used with the Kelly technique and began using it instead of mu or nothingness. I tended to focus my eyes on my forehead instead of straight ahead because of my previous experience. With these changes, I obtained good results practically from the first night. I never tried Zen or any other type of meditation during the daytime, except occasionally as a prelude to a daytime nap.

Daytime naps were always easy for me because I set a twenty to thirty minute maximum duration. With this short duration, I could collapse into sleep without thought of the future or the past nearly everytime. I focussed my eyes upward and thought black. During high school I began the habit of reviewing the day and planning the next day. This habit still interferes with going to sleep at night, but does not interfere with entering into a short nap.

Autogenic training was slow to arrive in the United States. From my first awareness of it, it appealed to me because of its concept of destroying detrimental attitudes and habits and establishing desirable ones. Verbalization of self-suggestion objectives seemed to me to be one more persuasive force to direct the brain into sleep. The self-suggestions seemed a more effective way to produce sleep than a meaningless mantra or a nothingness concept. I found it easier to hold my concentration on an understandable, persuasive suggestion than on the vagueness of meditation. I also felt comforted by suggestions when I was agitated.

The last classification of sleep techniques that I undertook to learn was self-hypnotism. After having learned the practice of self-suggestion in autogenic training, self-hypnosis seemed simple and familiar. Both self-hypnosis and autogenic training seek to reach the subconscious mind in order to get it to direct the conditions that produce sleep. I found self-hypnosis for sleep easy to accept because I could see that, in a crude way, I had been trying the same practice nearly every day without using the more effective technique.

The other methods for producing sleep seem to contain mainly the elements found in various combinations of the Jacobson, Kelly, autogenic training and meditation methods. Any of them are effective. There is no best way for everyone. The specific technique you develop will ultimately be yours alone, different in some detail from that of anyone else. My system works for my own experience, attitude, habits, emotions and senses.

The research that has been developed has been directed at four of the five senses. I find it curious that no attempt has been made to enlist the sense of smell in inducing sleep. The sense of smell is recognized by everyone as a mood maker, particularly as it relates to food and perfume. It might also have something to do with the mood for sleep.

We all seek to change our existence in order to be more comfortable, effective, attractive or influential. These aims require us to shed interfering habits and to control our thoughts and attention. If we do this we will attain our objectives more easily and quickly. This result is one of the by-products which has come to me from the practice and discipline of learning sleep control. Such exercise of your will should do as much for you.